A THOUSAND TRIBES

A THOUSAND TRIBES

HOW TECHNOLOGY UNITES PEOPLE IN GREAT COMPANIES

Robin Lissak and George Bailey

John Wiley & Sons, Inc.

Published by John Wiley & Sons, Inc., New York.
Published simultaneously in Canada.

Book Design: MGT Design

This publication is designed to provide accurate and authoritative information in regard to the subject matter covered. It is sold with the understanding that the publisher is not engaged in rendering professional services. If professional advice or other expert assistance is required, the services of a competent professional person should be sought.

Designations used by companies to distinguish their products are often claimed as trademarks. In all instances where John Wiley & Sons, Inc., is aware of a claim, the product names appear in initial capital or ALL CAPITAL LETTERS. Readers, however, should contact the appropriate companies for more complete information regarding trademarks and registration.

ISBN 0-471-22283-6

Printed in the United States of America

10 9 8 7 6 5 4 3 2 1

To our wives and families

Dedicated to all the PwC Partners and Consultants and their clients who are pushing the frontiers of technology ever outward, while at the same time bringing people around the world closer together. Without them, our book would only be about theory. With their contribution, our book is about the emerging future.

Contents

Foreword

Lately, it's seemed tough to rally support for investment in organizational change. The shattering scope of world events coupled with massive upheaval in the economy has left people seeking solace and safety in the status quo. In the face of continuous layoffs, corporate scandals, CEO failures, bankruptcy filings, travel uncertainties, and anxieties over terrorism, mere survival seems an accomplishment. But the status quo is as unacceptable today as at anytime in business history. When downturns reverse course, as inevitably happens, and hope is restored, the best companies will be ready with imaginative new responses. As a Harvard Business School professor and expert on leadership and innovation, I know change is hard and can sometimes hurt, so it is all too tempting to avoid it. That would be a mistake. Significant, paradigm-shifting change lies ahead, even in these challenging times. The driving force is technology: the still-unfolding possibilities offered by the Internet.

That's the rationale for this book—to help companies get ready for change to an Internet-enabled future. *A Thousand Tribes* describes companies in the midst of sweeping makeovers; they are taking work that has been done almost the same way for the past 50 years and moving it to the web. Of course, the Internet and the web were at the heart of the dot-com hysteria and left many people with a sour taste after the dot-com bubble burst. But the truth is that the Internet is in its infancy, only just becoming a powerful force for change. Now that the unrealistic hype about the Internet has died, the promise of the Internet can emerge.

In today's economy, for example, all organizations need greater reach. They need to be in more places, to be more aware of regional and cultural differences, and to integrate into coherent strategies the work occurring in different markets and communities. The advent of the Internet and the world wide web over the past decade has provided the means to achieve greater reach at greater speed, and to work more closely with customers and suppliers in the process.

Companies also require ways to reduce infrastructure costs, spur innovation, respond more quickly to market shifts, and enhance the value of their greatest assets, their people. To be effective in their work, people need to feel connected to a community of colleagues, yet also to feel that their personal needs and interests can be understood and expressed. All of this is made possible in new ways through the Internet. Businesses are just beginning to explore the opportunities and invent the new models.

In my recent book, *Evolve!*, I noted that mastering this environment requires evolving to a new way of working, a new way of doing business, a new style of human relationships. "The Web rewards organizations that are nimble and innovative, with a freer spirit of creation," I observed, "ones that can move quickly because all the right connections are in place. That need for agility has been noted frequently. What has not been examined is the Web's hidden secret: that it provokes a shift toward more collaborative work relationships, ones that resemble open, inclusive communities more than they resemble secretive hierarchical administrative bureaucracies."

As Robin Lissak and George Bailey point out in this book, the Internet is finally at a point of technological and cultural acceptance that makes effective online collaborative work relationships a growing reality. In the authors' case study companies, powerful and ubiquitous portals are spawning new communities both within and outside organizations, linking people around the office, the country, and the globe in ways that were once unthinkable.

By moving many tasks to the web, companies can accrue numerous benefits: speed, influence, innovation, and considerable cost savings. What the authors call business to *everything* (B2E), is at the core of a new organizational structure. Business to everything is not a cosmetic change or a program du jour; it represents a fundamental shift in the way organizations interact with employees, customers, suppliers, and partners. Companies are moving in this direction because staying in place means falling behind.

But despite the remarkable power and capability of this technology, organizations need more than web sites and faster servers to make it work. In a global, high-tech world, organizations need to be more fluid, inclusive, and responsive. They need to manage complex information flows, grasp new ideas quickly, and spread those ideas throughout the enterprise. What counts is not whether everybody uses e-mail, but whether people quickly absorb the impact of information and respond to opportunity.

As with the early stages of any major technological transformation, we are constricted by the absence of things today that will be taken for granted tomorrow. In 2002, for example, many organizations have not yet given all employees access to the Internet. Providing high-speed, broadband connections along with simple, intuitive interfaces continues to be an issue at many large corporations. Matters of privacy, security, and ethical conduct are all still on the table, even as the change itself is in full motion.

Yet the technology and even the policy issues are often the easy part; the harder part is the human side, the challenges of leading change. My years of study and experience show that while bold strokes—courageous decisions by leaders—can trigger change, it takes long marches—independent, discretionary, and ongoing efforts of people throughout the organization—to sustain change long enough to produce tangible results. No matter how the technology advances, these efforts remain at the heart of any organizational transformation. Organizations, after all, are collections of people. Company performance is built on how people interact, how they communicate a message to customers, and how they carry forward a corporate agenda and make it profitable and sustainable.

I believe that we are now at the outset of a long march toward a new kind of workplace. This book offers an inside look at how this long march is proceeding at several bellwether organizations, including Hewlett-Packard (HP), Ford Motor Company, Pricewaterhouse-Coopers (PwC), and the British Broadcasting Corporation (BBC). The "thousand tribes" of unconnected people and departments the authors have encountered at all of these organizations are quite familiar to me. In my work with companies struggling with change, I have documented the innovation-stifling, performance-reducing impact of tribes defending their turf, clinging to territory, and protecting rather than sharing information. And I have seen the ways in which corporate leaders have addressed the often-daunting issue of bringing these tribes together into an effective, cohesive organization. That's where the promise of B2E applications can play a role.

Lissak and Bailey take us on a tour through ongoing B2E initiatives. Along the way, they provide insights from the leaders of these complex efforts who must piece together coherent strategies even though resistance to change can pop up anywhere. The authors do not sugar-coat the difficulties of being at the front of a new trend. Their case study organizations are still struggling with the implementation of these staggering changes, and at least one CEO has been lost along the way. But within these struggles are lessons for other CEOs and senior managers who understand that this is the same long march their own organizations must undertake.

To guide transformation and create one enterprise out of disparate, sometimes warring, tribes, a new kind of leader is required. Obsolete tenets of leadership, steeped in the traditions of hierarchical organizational structure (e.g., the idea that a leader can be some sort of new-age Wizard of Oz, operating behind a curtain of obscurity) are no longer valid or effective. In a successful B2E environment, corporate chieftains must lead out in the open on an electronic stage that places them in a more visible role than ever before.

I have long argued that open, inclusive communities are a hallmark of corporate culture for high-performance, high-innovation companies. Creating such communities within large, traditional corporate entities is a scary proposition for many executives. Some leaders are happier as *cheer*leaders, touting the good news, diluting the bad news. Yet the fear factor is likely to be mitigated by the growing realization that the Enron model of closed cultures, communication roadblocks, and secretive actions in the executive suite is simply unacceptable in the B2E age.

If organizations of the twenty-first century are to become effective, open communities, their leaders will need role models and lessons like those in this book. And they will need to invest in large-scale organizational change. To get big results, small piecemeal projects won't do the trick. It will take a coherent vision, the desire to innovate, and the courage to keep at it even when the challenges seem overwhelming. The best leaders recognize that when faced with difficult tasks, it's important to get first steps underway quickly, to provide early wins that demonstrate what's possible. In the words of one of the CEOs showcased here, "It's going to be hard, so let's just get on with it."

ROSABETH MOSS KANTER

(c) Copyright 2002 by Rosabeth Moss Kanter.

Special Acknowledgment

We would like to recognize the very special contribution of Carly Fiorina, who has graciously allowed us to use her quote, "A Thousand Tribes," as part of our title and has also provided us with valuable insights for the Hewlett-Packard case study.

Acknowledgments

To Jacques Nasser, retired CEO, Ford Motor Company; Peter White, director of financial operations for the BBC; and Tom Siebel, Chairman, Siebel Corporation—we extend our great appreciation for their assistance in the preparation of our case studies. We would also like to thank our clients Susan Bowick, Steven Rice, W. James Fish, David Cooper, Rajan Nagarajan, and David Erickson for helping to form our vision for B2E and working through the application of our concepts in business settings. Finally, we'd like to extend special thanks to our PwC colleagues Bob Bleimeister, Sara Longworth, Sam Berger, Greg Johnson, Frederick D. Miller, Graeme Butterworth, Tom Murnane, Lisa Tondreau, Jeff Altman, Joe Duffy, Terry Lister, John Simke, Wendy Roy, Ken Campbell, Edna Diez, Philippe Houssiau, Richard Stanger, Herbert Nathan, Richard Dunsdon, Cathy Neuman, James Alvilhiera, Joel Kurtzman, Roger Lipsey, Arden Melick, and Bob Finnis—their energy and involvement helped make this book possible.

A THOUSAND TRIBES

Introduction: Encountering a Thousand Tribes

Picture this: You are the CEO of a large corporation and your mandate over the past half-dozen years has been to globalize your company and leverage size and scale in unprecedented ways. The future, you believe, belongs to dominant multinational players who successfully integrate technology and strategy in order to fuel global growth, reduce costs, spur innovation, and unleash true competitive advantage.

Business is about people. If you are Ford Motor Company, this means uniting 350,000 employees in 160 countries. At PricewaterhouseCoopers (PwC), it means 150,000 consultants in 150 countries. For Hewlett-Packard (HP), the count is 90,000 employees in 127 countries. The British Broadcasting Corporation (BBC) has 23,000 full-time and 15,000 contract freelancers scattered around the globe. And though the concept is compelling, the reality is daunting. Becoming global means undoing decades' worth of management wisdom and organizational structure in order to truly take advantage of international marketplaces. After more than a decade of embracing the doctrine of decentralization and autonomous business units, you are forced to rethink the very way that work gets done.

So ingrained has autonomy become in our corporate hierarchies that when Carleton S. (Carly) Fiorina became CEO at HP in 1999, she discovered, among those 90,000 employees in 127 countries, a company of what she calls "a thousand tribes," referring to countless autonomous business units that had each created their own set of rules on how to do business. "What happened over time was that everybody rolled their own," Fiorina says. "Everybody went off and did their own thing on everything."

Ford, PwC, and the rest of the Fortune 1000 companies all had their thousand tribes scattered around the globe. As the alleged new economy got underway, CEOs everywhere realized that such fractionalized organizations would never be able to compete effectively without transformational change across the entire company. What was needed was a way to reunite the organization without diluting the power of the individual. What was required were new and creative ways to draw power and strategy from the Internet, which had emerged as the obvious thread to tie together the company of the future. Now, people connect to people in ways that were previously unthinkable, thereby increasing their effectiveness exponentially. Getting there, however, is clearly going to require new ways to lead and manage. Getting there is going to require the embrace of the Internet in ways that heretofore have not been fully explored. Most big companies have spent the past five years figuring out the killer Bs—B2C (business to consumer), B2B (business to business), and B2E (business to employee). But these have been incremental steps, baby steps in a world that requires giant strides in order to move ahead quickly.

We believe in a broader concept in which B2E means business to *everything*. This B2E goes beyond the limited Internet connections thus far explored and implemented with varying degrees of success. Business to everything is,

in fact, the catalyst to this transformational change across
the organization. It is about moving work to the web via
powerful new portals, thus transforming not only companies but individuals, not only work lives but personal lives,
by leveraging people, process, technology, and culture.

CHANGING THE NATURE OF WORK

If you really examine it, the nature of work has not
changed significantly over the last 20 years. *What* we do
has not been redefined by *how* we do it, despite the dramatic technological revolution that we've experienced over
the past two decades. Managers still oversee groups of
workers, guiding them and grading them using much the
same metrics as in the past. Accountants still count. Purchasing agents still purchase. Recruiters still recruit. Those
in human resources still administer health benefits, retirement plans, and employee stock options. And on and on.

Obviously, the advent of personal computers, high-
speed networks, telecommunications, e-mail, personal
digital assistants, cellular phones, and the Internet, have
markedly changed the way we do our work and where we
do it. Can anyone imagine a cashier punching in numbers
on a cash register, a writer still using a typewriter, or a
layout designer shipping page proofs through the mail?

Yet we are forced to wonder if all we've done is
speed the plow and pave the cow path, essentially doing
the same things we used to do, only faster with fewer
errors. While this is not necessarily a bad thing, it certainly begs the question of whether the hundreds of billions of dollars of technology spending over these two
decades has raised the proverbial bar all that much
higher? Have we significantly improved productivity
across a vast range of industries? Have we dramatically
lowered costs or spurred innovation? Have we truly
increased quality in the goods and services we make and

sell and, perhaps more important, improved the quality of the lives of our employees, our customers, and ourselves?

Nearly a decade ago, Michael Hammer and James Champy set off a widespread and chaotic rethinking of corporate America with their breakthrough best-seller, *Reengineering the Corporation*. In it, the authors urged American companies not to try to fix the outmoded business processes still in place since Adam Smith's *The Wealth of Nations* was published in 1776, but to instead start over from scratch—"don't automate, obliterate!"—a powerful message that sent most CEOs into a panic mode of restructuring and downsizing.[1] Though the authors never intended for their concept to become the linchpin for massive layoffs and utter confusion inside corporations, more often than not, that is what happened.

Perhaps the widespread misunderstanding was caused by the drastic nature of the authors' ideas. Demanding that giant, global, multi-billion-dollar organizations toss out every existing business process and start again might have been more than most corporate cultures could bear. Or perhaps the authors formulated their thinking too soon. The advent of the Internet and the world wide web, which appeared just a few short years after the book was published, surely would have had a significant impact on the very nature of reengineering.

We believe reengineering's demise was a combination of these two shortcomings, plus another: The authors misunderstood the nature of work and underestimated the difficulties companies face in trying to make themselves over. There are so many mitigating factors outside the walls of every corporation that impact the work inside that simple formulas for change are unlikely to spawn the desired results. In the so-called new economy, markets shift and trends come and go at lightning speed, global forces now commandeer local initiatives, and world-shaking events like the September 11 terrorist attacks can undermine even the most thoughtful, carefully executed business plans. The global recession that began seemingly overnight in 2001 arrived with a swiftness and severity that none but the most robust corporate strategies could have overcome.

Reengineering also failed to recognize the need for personalization of the workplace, where each employee can make a unique contribution. The standardized business processes that reengineering produced neglected to take into account the advent of mass customization that enables every employee to innovate and contribute in a personal way. If reengineering accomplished anything, it was to turn senior business executives into cynics about oversimplified prescriptions for corporate success. Though it put hardly a dent in the sales of how-to business books, it certainly caused CEOs to think twice about shamans bearing life-saving programs du jour.

We don't blame the CEOs. Having lived through the wild fluctuations of the world economy over the past few years, we understand that the new-millennium CEO has a job exponentially tougher than his or her predecessors.

Indeed, as the new millennium got underway, the chieftains of global business found themselves in an oddly uncomfortable and unfamiliar place. After several decades of both welcoming and dreading technology's reinvention of the corporate world, CEOs yearned for the birth of a new era, a golden age where the marriage of business and information technology (IT) would finally deliver on the much-hyped promise that had bombarded them for years.

Instead, the new era arrived rather dismally. The massive fear and spending triggered by the mostly unfounded Y2K scare was followed quickly by the crashing end of the dot-com revolution. Having observed in shock and astonishment the rise of the well-documented dot-com, start-up frenzy—the remarkable run-up in valuation of virtual online companies without products, profits, or occasionally even a business plan—corporate leaders in traditional organizations felt vaguely unsettled about where to place their technology bets moving forward.

After all, these same CEOs had signed off on billions spent on a laundry list of technology initiatives, only to discover the enormous difficulty in implementing and profiting from such expenditures. Return on investment has always been a nebulous concept within the walls of the IT organization, and the rush to the Internet during the dot-com era created more skeptics than champions.

In the aftermath of the dot-com boom, many questioned the very validity of the Internet, likening it to the tulip wars or the California gold rush. No sooner did the dot-com fiasco slip out of the headlines than the global economy nose-dived as well. With breathtaking speed, the once robust spending on IT dried up. CEOs decided it was a good time to stop and reflect on the billions of dollars that had been funneled into corporate IT infrastructures for years and years. "What is the return on this massive investment?" many asked in frustration.

The slowdown in spending set off pandemonium in the high-tech sector. High-flying players in every segment— from Cisco Systems, Lucent, and Nortel to EMC, Compaq, and Intel—saw share prices tumble and quarterly earnings disappear with startling quickness. Corporate layoffs washed over the industry like a typhoon as daily headlines reported cutbacks of tens of thousands of workers. Like dominoes, the giants toppled one after another.

While many CEOs lingered on the sidelines feeling as if they'd emerged from one state of chaos directly into the next, a few savvy leaders saw opportunity in the tumult. As Thomas L. Friedman wrote in the *New York Times,*

The Internet isn't tulips, and if you think it is, well, let's talk in five years. By then it will be clear that the Internet is a business evolution— reshaping how businesses communicate, educate, and purchase materials; a social revolution— connecting people who have never been connected before; and for both of these reasons, a strategic dilemma that we are just beginning to understand.[2]

CONNECTING THE PRESENT TO THE FUTURE

What we've seen in working with dozens of large companies over the past two years is that the time has come to transform the nature of work and how it is done. The promise of reengineering is embodied in our concept of B2E but with a crucial and powerful difference. Now, the technology exists to move work to the web, and with this, companies are able to unlock and revitalize their intellectual capital, once considered an intangible asset. By moving work to the web, that asset becomes very tangible indeed.

Business to everything is not simply a tool to reduce your costs today, but a foundation for connecting the present to the future. It is about embracing the Internet to transform your business and the way you work. It is *not* a program du jour. If anything, it is a long, extended journey rather than a destination. This book is not intended to be a how-to for your business. Rather, it offers detailed glimpses into what we believe are fascinating and effective works in progress; glimpses intended to get you thinking about what your organization might look like or should look like as you navigate through one of the most turbulent business environments in our history. It is mostly about creating a strong channel of communication throughout a global organization; communication that moves instantly and directly from point to point, whether from the CEO to the assembly line worker, from manager to salaried staffer, or from peer to peer.

Most important, this is not simply a theory we've hit upon in the ozone of academia. We have been lucky enough to work with some of the world's most dynamic companies as they go through this transformational change. We have been privileged to help them implement B2E in ways that help them achieve their strategic goals. So this book illustrates where B2E is already in place and unfolding at dozens of companies around the world. The book is designed to provide you with several case study examples of B2E at work, already instigating enormous change.

For example, when Carly Fiorina became chief executive officer at HP, she knew she was joining the venerable Silicon Valley giant at a crucial and troubling time in its history. Her job would not be that of a caretaker CEO; just the opposite, she would have to initiate and implement massive change to a company that had practically invented the modern high-technology industry.

Bringing 90,000 employees in 127 countries together in a corporate reinvention is a daunting task for even the most seasoned business leaders, and Fiorina encouraged new kinds of thinking from all corners of the company. What she found at HP, she says, were those "thousand tribes" all following their own autonomous sets of rules based loosely upon the vaunted HP Way. At the center of her vision was the creation of an ambitious enterprise-wide portal that would harness the power of the Internet and literally change HP's world. The portal, which debuted in late 2000, is at the heart of HP's reinvention as a company. The portal now connects HP's employee population together in a way that was heretofore impossible, even at one of the world's most admired technology makers. When HP announced plans to acquire giant Compaq Computer Corporation in 2001, Fiorina was counting on the portal to play a crucial role in the integration of the two diverse corporate cultures.

You will learn in detail about HP's new portal in Chapter 3. As at our other in-depth case studies of Ford Motor Company, PwC, and the BBC, enterprise portals have emerged at the heart of B2E as the new central nervous system for companies seeking to remake themselves as new-millennium leaders in their industries. We have also included the voices of several CEOs of technology companies that are building the platforms that will drive the B2E revolution. Because they are instrumental in building corporate portals, their insights are valuable additions to our vision of the future. These portals, when well conceived and executed, initiate dramatic transformations in the way work gets done and how employees view the very intersection of their personal and professional lives.

The portal at HP is an example of the transformations we have seen. It accelerates the pace of work and connects nearly all computing devices—from desktops to PDAs—allowing people to work anywhere, anytime and share that work around the globe. It helps eliminate the middle person in the corporate bureaucracy and does away with much of the bureaucracy itself. It creates the opportunity for sharing tools and exchanging ideas; in fact, it sets up a completely different way of working. Because it provides for the very first time a way to connect everyone in the company with everyone else, the portal embodies and makes real the inventive spirit that technologists have envisioned for several decades. It does nothing less than transform the *promise* of the Internet into the *reality* of a worldwide network that is fast, powerful, secure, and personal.

More than anything, however, the portal is the key to B2E. Business to everything is the concept designed to bring the Internet inside, to employees, and allow them to work and conduct business more efficiently. Not surprisingly, B2E had its roots in the human resources function and was usually dismissed as a needed but mundane path that companies must trod.

But in working with hundreds of clients through the chaotic late 1990s and into the new millennium, we began to see a clear pattern emerge: B2E was nothing if not the next corporate Trojan horse. Rather than seeing B2E as a way to embrace corporate intranets, we met some remarkably smart and visionary people who understood that B2E can actually provide the catalyst to corporation transformation.

As you read this book, you will begin to understand how some very smart people in some very powerful companies are embracing B2E to fundamentally shift the nature of work. You will read, for example, how Ford Motor Company gave every employee a new personal computer, printer, and Internet access for their homes in order to increase the Internet literacy of its workforce and impact both their work and personal lives. Ford doesn't expect and hasn't requested any financial measure or return on this multi-million-dollar investment. Ford believes that a literate and intelligent workforce is a prerequisite to successfully doing business in the new millennium.

We believe Ford "gets" the Internet and the potency of B2E. We hope that as you read the following chapters, you will find such thinking infectious and inspiring, as we have.

CHAPTER ONE

Preparing for the B2E Revolution

He that will not apply new remedies must expect new evils; for time is the greatest innovator.
—Francis Bacon[1]

Like nature, business is both cyclical and unpredictable. Trying to learn from business history is fraught with peril because, despite conventional wisdom, little that has happened before is likely to be relevant today—especially today.

It would have been virtually impossible, for example, to predict the unprecedented run of prosperity through much of the 1990s after a recessionary period early in the decade. And it would have been even more difficult to foresee the great dot-com bubble of the late 1990s and the incredibly swift fall in the global markets that began with the new millennium.

Certainly there have been intense periods of innovation before. The late nineteenth century brought us world-changing inventions such as the telegraph, the lightbulb, the phonograph, the radio, the telephone, the automobile, the diesel engine, and the airplane, to name a few. These wondrous technologies set off equally intense periods of investment. As the *New York Times* recently noted, "From 1900 to 1925, there were more than 3000 automobile startups in America turning out cars of every imaginable design. Some had six wheels, others had ship like tillers for steering."[2]

Knowing this did nothing to squelch the investment fever that gripped the marketplace in the late 1990s and resulted in 18-month-old Internet start-ups with greater market values than General Motors and AT&T. Sometimes the business world sees only what it wants to see, and separating truth and value from hype can be a challenge.

What we *can* learn is that the business climate inevitably shifts over time and produces giddy heights and frightening troughs that are not for the fainthearted. We also see that for companies to successfully maneuver through these monumental shifts, new remedies are indeed required.

This book is about new remedies that offer something more valuable than turnkey solutions and new business jargon. For the past five years, we have helped companies rethink and remake the way people work, communicate, and connect with customers, suppliers, and each other. What we've learned and want to share with you is a way for organizations to *get prepared* for these inevitable shifts and slides that are part of business reality and to create an effective means to handle the inevitable changes without losing their balance.

Getting prepared does not mean tearing out multi-million-dollar technology investments and replacing them with other multi-million-dollar investments. If anything, the companies we've worked with have actually activated past technology investments in ways that top executives have been asking for the past decade. In so doing, companies are finally embracing the Internet and unleashing its potential both within and outside the organization. We will show you, in a series of case studies, how some of our biggest and most successful client companies are laying the groundwork today for a time in the not-so-distant future when the Internet will not only fundamentally transform the way they work, but will become as ubiquitous and unobtrusive as electricity and telephones.

BUSINESS TO EVERYTHING

If the advent of new technologies has done nothing else, it has increased the speed of business and of business cycles to unprecedented levels. These technologies, from personal computers to the Internet, have spawned not so much a new economy as new economics, a delicate and imprecise science with few true visionaries.

Even the great business icons of the day like Warren Buffett, Bill Gates, and Jack Welch are hard-pressed to make sense of it all. And despite all the signs that we have entered a new era of innovation and organizational dynamics, companies continue to reach for yesterday's responses to today's business crises.

In the midst of the current recession, for example, as industries have rushed to consolidate and as individual companies respond to anemic quarterly earnings numbers with massive cutbacks and layoffs, we wonder how we are to move out beyond these cycles if all we do is drastically downsize. You may eliminate some of the thousands of tribes that make up large corporations, but you will not resolve the underlying need to link the remaining tribes together in a coherent fashion.

We have spent a good portion of our careers studying the way people work and, while we understand the need to reduce costs in hard economic times, we wonder whether most top executives are too focused on short-term financials rather than on changing the way work is actually done.

We believe that we are at the threshold of a dramatic

remaking of business. We know you've heard that before. We understand your skepticism. We have spent the past two decades struggling with organizational and technological cataclysms that generally served to confuse rather than catalyze vast improvements in either bottom-line results or people's satisfaction with their lives. But now we have the confluence of several key elements—technology, bandwidth, and visionary thinking—that can actually change the way people work and the nature of the work itself.

Here is why:

→ The Internet is finally robust enough and accessible enough to allow companies to move significant work to the web.

→ Well-designed and carefully implemented enterprise portals are set to become the information arteries of global corporations, capable of reducing costs, driving new revenue, and helping to retain valuable employees, customers, and suppliers.

→ By embracing this new technology, companies can effectively and dramatically change not only the nature of work but also the integration of people's work and personal lives.

We have spent the past several years working with clients on the concept of *business to everything* (B2E). We have helped dozens of Fortune 1000 companies build and implement B2E portals, and we have seen impressive results already, not only in reducing costs in the short term, but in providing an important foundation for the future of the company.

To each of these companies, B2E means slightly different things. But at its heart, B2E is the means by which companies can finally and fully become connected using the Internet as the platform and enterprise portals as the vehicle to reach everyone, everywhere. In some ways, the term *portal* is misleading. *Portal* implies a wall that has been penetrated. What we're talking about here is actually the whole landscape of possibilities beyond the portal.

WELCOME TO THE AGE OF NO-NONSENSE BUSINESS

According to the *New York Times,* the "economically significant assimilation" of the Internet has begun, "but experts believe its impact will continue to spread over the next decade or more." The *New York Times* cited an 18-month Brookings Institute study[3] that predicts the impact of Internet technology will add one-quarter to one-half percentage point annually to the productivity growth of the U.S. economy over the next five years.

"Economically, the Internet is just like electricity," Robert E. Litan, director of economic studies at Brookings told the *New York Times.* "First, it's new and exciting. Then it steadily transforms your economy. And decades later, nobody would think to call it the 'electricity economy.' It's just there."

What we are seeing in our last few years out in the trenches is perhaps best characterized as the end of the beginning. Finally, a few courageous companies are committed to their own transformation. To us, this is the culmination of the Internet era when the fits and starts are actually coming together into exciting, implementable plans, and companies are figuring out how to personalize work and reach literally everyone.

Within their grasp at long last is a way to integrate the endless disparate systems and technologies that have turned corporations into confusing disconnected grids over the past 15 years. Perhaps the most appealing aspect of B2E is that it does not require obliterating existing investments for even more expensive new investments.

What business leader hasn't been frustrated by his or her company's agonizingly slow response to market changes? What business leader has not gnashed his or her teeth at the escalating costs of technology implementations over the past decade?

Yet we may finally be arriving at a point in technology history where the tools are available and the timing is right to turn the hype into reality. Tom Siebel, the founder and CEO of Siebel Systems, the $2 billion software vendor, is running his entire company on the web using his own products to dramatically shift the way business is done. It is more than simple vendor hype to have 8,000 employees in 134 offices in 35 countries run one of the fastest-growing companies in the United States almost completely online.

Siebel's internal use of the Internet has impacted literally every process—from budgeting to performance reviews—and turned the organization into a flexible, focused team that is capable of reacting swiftly to shifting market needs. More than anything else, Siebel's portal communicates and reinforces the company's corporate culture across the entire organization, and this has a powerful influence over people's behavior.

We've observed that companies facing difficult economic times tend to hedge their bets or hesitate in the hopes that a solution will offer itself up from trendsetters in other industries. Business leaders must ask themselves, "Are we going to sell our way out of this? Are we going to just do the same thing we've done and pray for a miracle or work in a radically different way?"

We believe there is a cheaper, far more effective, public alternative. It's called the Internet. By moving work to the web, companies can finally activate their past technology investments. But unlike in the past, where every new technology trend was maddeningly incompatible with what was already in place, B2E does not require you to rip out your infrastructure and start again with a new $65 million technology implementation.

What we find is that many executives believe their companies have already moved work to the web. When we first began working with Hewlett-Packard (HP) for example, we suggested moving human resources (HR) processes like recruiting online and we were told, "Oh, we've already done that." We asked about penetration and utilization and we were told, "We don't measure that." When we checked the portal, we discovered they still had multiple channels around the company, and people could not figure out how to navigate through the system. The result was that people weren't using the Internet as HP had believed.

At the pharmaceutical giant GlaxoSmithKline, Elaine Davis, vice president of HR Strategy, Communications & Systems, says her big struggle, and one we've seen at many companies, is that most functional groups within companies have created their own web sites and view the portal as simply a way to link those sites together. "They don't seem to understand that a true portal experience for the employee would be having the ability to pick and choose content without regard to who owns it," Davis says. "The technology is way ahead of the organization's ability to deal with it."

Indeed, this isn't restricted to portal technology. We often find that companies have invested millions into technology implementations, and people aren't using it. They've made the investment, but it hasn't changed the way people do their work.

We met with Glaxo as they were merging with Smith Kline Beecham. They said to us, "We're merging. Our stock price is falling as we're merging, and we don't want to make any new investments in systems. What can we do?" What they wanted was to use the web to help with the merger process. They wanted a portal that employees from both companies could access to find out more about the new company and what their specific jobs would be. Who would they report to? Who would report to them? What will the company sell?

They expected us to tell them, "What you need to do is build a new house, put in a new foundation, and put new plumbing in place." Instead, we said, "It's not about that. It's about a person's experience and finding a way to deliver information to that person." We suggested overlaying an enterprise-wide portal over their current systems with the idea that it would grow eventually into a true B2E environment.

There was neither time nor money to merge two HR systems or two payroll systems into one. This was a perfect opportunity for B2E, because companies have spent the past 20 years putting all this expensive infrastructure in place but haven't focused on the delivery and the integration of work as it relates to the individual. The Internet enables us to activate those expensive investments in a way that we simply haven't done up to now.

At the same time, companies gain the ability to finally resolve the centralized versus the decentralized paradox that has haunted CEOs for more than a decade. In essence, B2E offers the best of both worlds—the classic loose/tight organization—by putting the power of technology in the hands of the people while, at the same time, allowing tight standards to be implemented across the organization.

With the full power of the Internet in hand, we now see a single media channel that is driving change. No longer are companies going to be dependent on managing a host of different environments such as PCs, personal digital

assistants (PDAs), laptops, and cell phones. No longer will
people need multiple logons to access different parts of the
organization. This intersection of work lives and personal
lives will spread e-literacy and ease the technoconfusion
that has curbed our enthusiasm for this new age.

In an age when business cycles can shift in a matter
of weeks or months rather than years, it is more difficult
but more crucial than ever to create one company and
one message. As consolidation touches nearly every major
industry, the need for a globally connected organization is
paramount. Though it is more possible than ever before,
it remains a difficult challenge.

Yet what is the residual value when everything is
connected? Look back through the industrial age and
every major leap forward in communication—the telegraph, the railroad, the telephone, the radio, television,
and then computers—produced an enormous hike in the
value and speed of information.

The Internet is yet another exponential leap forward.
We've not seen anything like it, and we have yet to harness its full potential. But we believe that B2E is the
broad concept that will allow companies to do just that.
Despite all of the advances in communications just mentioned, never before now have we had a world that is
truly connected in this way. The implications for the
transformation of work are staggering. And with it, the
age of no-nonsense business begins.

In the earliest days of a new technology, few have the
benefit of distance and time to anticipate the potential
and to savor the rewards. Yet when we've worked with
clients on B2E and created clear strategic visions, implementable plans to move forward, and both short-term
and long-term goals that are fully attainable, something
amazing happens.

"The reason B2E is happening now is that we are entering an age when intangible assets like human capital and intellectual capital drive business success[,] and B2E is the way to grow both forms of capital," says David M. Erickson, vice president of HR shared services at Pfizer, Inc.

At the $30 billion Pfizer, the world's largest pharmaceutical company, with 85,000 employees in 150 countries, the ingredients are in place for B2E. "We have achieved the goal of becoming the number one company in the pharmaceuticals industry so we had to set a new goal, which is to become the world's most valued company. In order to do that, we must focus on connecting people to create value," Erickson says.

What Erickson observed is that Pfizer was already prepared in many ways for B2E but simply didn't know it. This is a scenario we've discovered at many companies. "We recognize that B2E is inevitable," Erickson says. "We just have to figure out how to make it happen. All the elements are here. We have had a lot of web applications built within functional and business unit groups, but now have a new governance structure that builds constituencies and connections across those boundaries." Through that governance structure, Pfizer is defining how to service and connect its employees.

Pfizer held a "share fair," for example, and discovered a raft of best practices around the firm that most people did not know about. By moving work to the portal, these best practices—in finance, in HR, in research and development—could be shared around the globe, Erickson points out.

In this book, we will provide some very detailed looks at several companies, including our own, that have plunged feet-first into the B2E era. Though each story is unique to that particular company, the theme running through all these tales of transition is, How do companies effectively move work to the web and thus transform themselves in the process?

Today's CEOs are seeking a pivot point to move their companies forward, and we believe this is that point. CEOs have long been asking employees to accelerate, and they've also been asking for payback on their vast technology investments. We believe B2E is about fully activating and leveraging the investments that companies have already made. This is about technology that acts as a central artery for an organization, reaching everywhere and making work both personal and ubiquitous at the same time.

HOW DID WE GET HERE?

The advent of the world wide web in the mid-1990s will undoubtedly be regarded as a defining moment on any business timeline. Not surprising, the early years of the web were more hype and promise than reality as companies struggled to find a value proposition for this intriguing new communications channel.

Big companies struggled most of all. Because the Internet and the web are, essentially, software, the medium is programmable, which is both its strength and its weakness. By 1998, for example, most companies had a raft of employees familiar with HyperText Markup Language (HTML), the ubiquitous web programming language. Armed with this relatively easy-to-use capability, web sites were being built faster than anthills in a grassy backyard.

According to Michael Crosno, CEO of Epicentric, a leading enterprise portal software company, the average Fortune 2000 corporation built between 250 and 1,000 web sites. Kaiser Permanente, for example, had 350 web sites. J. P. Morgan Chase & Co., had 1,000 web sites. Any group or individual with a work-related agenda could, and did, post a site. There were indeed organizations with a thousand tribes all across corporate America and around the globe.

Amazingly, Crosno says, it was these independent, unconnected, unsupported web sites on which companies began to run their businesses. Though companies always had one or two main customer-facing web sites up and running, it was these independent internal intranets that ruled the day. Employees built them because they were dissatisfied with the main web sites and felt they could do better on their own. From this, the enterprise portal began to evolve.

Most companies began with business-to-employee intranets intended to serve HR functions. These were the most risk-free Crosno says because they were not available to business partners or customers outside the organization, and so they didn't risk embarrassing failure in the open world. Naturally, as these intranets proliferated, people added more and more functionality, and more tabs began to appear across the top of the home page. Thus, the single portal serving all began to implode under its own weight with too many tabs. A cluttered and crowded site becomes too difficult to navigate and people simply stop using it. B2E solves the single-channel issue and provides a powerful framework for moving work to the web in an organized manner.

In a 2001 report on enterprise portals, Forrester Research, a leading information technology (IT) research firm in Cambridge, Massachusetts, reported that while portals can be well worth the effort, they are not easy to build. A survey by Forrester of Global 3500 firms revealed that most current portal projects lack: a real financial justification, a real financial justification, a clear mission, an appropriate balance between business and IT, and a way to ensure employees that portals are not just the latest IT fad.

With all that said, Forrester is a strong proponent of portals and so are we. According to Forrester, big companies "have got the portal bug," and most are spending significant sums to build them across their enterprises. A Delphi Group report in 2001 showed that 75 percent of Global 1000 companies polled had already begun or planned to begin investing in portal technology by the end of the year. Another 13 percent were planning similar investments in 2002. We have seen firsthand what Forrester discovered in a recent portal survey of Global 3500 companies: When asked what the biggest portal challenge is, 71 percent replied "organizational issues."

Beyond that, we've learned firsthand a simple truth: You cannot underestimate how difficult the B2E transformation is, no matter how intuitive it might seem. The British Broadcasting Corporation (BBC), for example, has an entrenched culture that is based almost entirely on the whims of individual producers and managers. Introducing and enforcing the new financial portal on this idiosyncratic population has met with great skepticism and resistance. Companies heading down this path must create and follow a strategic vision. We bring up the old adage, "If you don't know where you are going, any direction will do." That is a recipe for disaster in a B2E implementation because at the end of the day, B2E is about getting people to change their behavior and how they think about both work and nonwork. Our colleague at PwC Consulting, John Allison, worked with Health Net, a $10 billion health services company, on their employee portal.

"How do you get people to recognize that this is very tough and it requires very powerful work? It requires resources and it is not just going to happen by somebody cranking out a memo," Allison said. "One of the tough lessons we learned at Health Net is that it takes longer than you thought and it is harder than you thought. But it was worth it."

In this book, you will read about both the trauma and the triumph of building a B2E portal. Though this is a technology-laden implementation, B2E at its heart is not about technology at all, but about organizational transformation. From our work, we believe B2E:

→ Allows a company to change its work processes

→ Allows a company to change the way it is organized to do work

→ Changes the relationship between the employee and the work

In essence, B2E is the catalyst for remaking an organization, and no company in business history has been reinvented without great pain and significant organizational angst.

"I don't think the problem in the enterprise as we move forward will be the *technology* of information management, but it really will be the *psychology* of information management," says Paul Gudonis, CEO of Genuity. "Because once you can get to any data that you need, then you have to make sure you think through what it is you really want to know and who you really want to share it with."

THE B2E VALUE PROPOSITION

In creating our framework for B2E, we discovered that companies that understand the concept and that are ready for this revolution exhibit four characteristics:

1. They understand that their strength comes from *knowledge,* not just from physical assets.

2. They understand that they must operate
   globally—effortlessly transferring ideas,
   people, and services from region to region.
3. They understand that *constant innovation* is
   their only defense against competition.
4. They realize that success in this new environment requires the *adroit use of informa-*
   tion to restructure an organization and
   boost productivity.

As you can see from the chart, shown in Figure 1.1, we
believe that B2E value is driven by multiple measures:

→ Hard cost savings

→ Real-time savings in business processes and
   personal productivity

B2E Value Proposition - Multiple Measures

Cost Savings	Innovation
Metric: Hard Cost Savings	**Metric: Increased Revenue**
• Headcount reduction	• Real-time collaboration
• Infrastructure reduction	• Better access to knowledge

Operational Efficiency	Employee Satisfaction
Metric: Time Savings	**Metric: Ease of Work**
• Streamlined processes	• Giving employees better tools
• Better access to information	• Making work easier
• Improved communications	• Creating better accessibility
• Cross-functional integration	

Providing strategic focus for infrastructure initiatives

**Figure 1.1   Multiple measures of the B2E value
proposition.**

→ Increased employee satisfaction—by making work easier, faster, better, and geographically unbounded

→ Potential for increased innovation, product development, and revenue generation

We've already seen companies achieve significant cost savings as they embark on B2E. Potential savings from web-enabling core business processes is at least 30 percent. Ford estimates that it saved $65 million in HR costs in 2001 alone. Oracle advertises that it saved $1 billion a year by moving work to the web. Hewlett-Packard holds that it is reducing 50 percent of its overall infrastructure costs with the B2E portal as the catalyst. Craig Conway, CEO of PeopleSoft, recalls a meeting with Jack Welch, now retired CEO of GE, at a CEO forum last year. Conway recalls Welch's discussion of the accomplishments at GE over the past several years. According to Welch, the most significant was the digitization of business processes, which resulted in billions of dollars in cost reduction. "I wrote down that quote and carry it around with me," recalls Conway.

Though some enterprise portal efforts suffer from lack of a clear return-on-investment (ROI) formula, we believe that a portal built within a true B2E setting can only scratch the surface of payback in its nascent stages. But moving work to the web will dramatically alter the bottom line as the effort reaches maturity.

Operational efficiency that results in real-time savings can be accomplished in two ways:

1. *Streamlined processes can effectively save vast amounts of time and add immeasurably to the quality of work being done.* Bringing in a new hire or a contractor,

for example, sets up a new dynamic. How fast can we teach this new person all the things they need to know about our organization so they become productive? If we can cut that time by two or three days, there is tremendous benefit to the organization.

2. *The other time savings are based upon better access to information.* Studies have shown that people in large organizations spend between one-half and two hours per day just looking for information. In one survey we received, people said their *primary job* is finding information. We all know what it's like to become information Sherpas, carrying and passing along information to others, which creates little or no value at all to the organization. You might feel good because you helped someone complete a task, but there's no inherent value in it. The value lies in giving each employee self-service capabilities so that the line between each of us and what we need to know is a straight and direct one.

A 2001 Hunter study found that 19 percent of companies had already implemented employee and managerial self-service transactions and that 71 percent of companies plan to add this functionality as they move forward.

The B2E portal dramatically alters the work/life environment. Jacques Nasser, Ford's retired CEO, understood this as he approved a plan to give every one of Ford's 350,000 employees a PC, printer, and Internet access from their homes. Ford had given out more than 150,000 of these packages to U.S. employees before putting the program on hold due to economic issues. However, by giving people tools to make their lives and their work easier, more accessible, and more fulfilling, companies stand a far better chance of retaining the best and brightest people and of improving overall employee satisfaction.

Employees tend to stay at a job for salary, for good management, for education, for exciting work, and for tools that make their lives better.

The U.S. Army, for example, is offering eligible enlisted soldiers an innovative e-learning opportunity via a global portal. The eArmyU portal allows soldiers to complete postsecondary degree programs online from anywhere in the world. A long list of accredited colleges and universities is participating with courseware and educators who instruct the courses entirely online. Access to this education opportunity caused 16 percent of eArmyU participants to reenlist in 2001 in order to be eligible for the program.

Finally, innovation is a by-product of the B2E revolution. Companies may actually develop products for internal use on the portal that can end up as a valuable offering to customers. And by organizing information better and connecting people more efficiently, we are seeing increased innovation in product development. At PwC, we created a web-based application that allowed consultants from all over the world to collaborate on innovative new ideas for their clients.

This is particularly true because of the potential for collaboration tools. In a global company, employees have counterparts all over the world. They want collaboration tools that will allow their projects to progress more quickly and effectively. At PeopleSoft, a software company with 9,000 employees in 36 countries, employees across the world have instantaneous access to business information anywhere, anytime through its B2E portal. Because the company runs its own collaborative business software, employees are able to access virtually any type of business application or information through any device that can access the Internet. They have access to and can share customer, company, finance, product, and HR information.

"Our employees require realtime access to business information to meet the demanding needs of our customers," said CEO Craig Conway, "and because everything we do is truly web based, we have a competitive advantage that allows us to quickly adopt and take advantage of new advances in technology. We're not dependent upon PCs, we can use any device that can access the Internet. We deliver realtime business information anywhere, anytime."

THE PORTAL AS ME

Using the portal, a veteran HP manager tells us she has done nothing less than reinvent her own career. She is no longer spending her days in a cubicle resolving disputes or tracking down information. Instead, she is able to work either from her office or from home and manage the careers of dozens of people, virtually none of whom work geographically nearby. She can do performance reviews, hire temporary employees, supervise critical projects, and invest time in her own personal interests—all via the portal.

The key to the effective use of the technology is *personalization*. Perhaps the most powerful and important aspect of B2E is that it allows employees to focus on "my experience, my work, and the communities that I care about." This kind of personalization is at the center of our B2E concept and represents the evolution we foresee within organizations. If you understand that people have long struggled with technology because it has consistently failed to embrace the way they organize their lives and their work, you can begin to understand why so many overhyped technology initiatives have failed over the past two decades.

Several years ago, we decided to introduce some of these concepts to Ford, one of our most important clients. And the first thing we had to do was find out how people would react to this kind of environment. What we discovered in our research was that people had a different frame of reference than we anticipated and that conventional wisdom dictated.

In focus groups, we asked Ford employees from different levels of the company how they would organize the business if they had technology that could tie the global company together. Rather than organizing by the traditional corporate model, which was to organize by function, people kept doing it "wrong." Or so we thought. Instead of dropping things within a nice corporate structure (i.e., HR, finance, IT, and other vertical functions), people used a completely different frame of reference: their own personal needs and desires. We thought we had done the focus groups wrong. Had we used the wrong methodology? Had we given incorrect instructions? We tried again and got the same reaction.

What people were telling us was simple and powerful: "I am the center of the universe when it comes to the web. I organize my world around me." That was the key. People weren't afraid to do it that way and, in fact, did it quite naturally.

If you create a model that is flexible enough to incorporate an individual's own personal needs into the technology, you can understand how to move work and business to the web. People want a single environment for work and home, an environment that is their own and one they can manage themselves. The essence of this model sounds like a tagline from a bad teen flick: *It's All about Me,* with a capital *M.*

Once the portal becomes about *me* and about the things *I* do and that are important to *me,* it becomes the internalization of what all leaders in organizations want to achieve. What leaders intrinsically want to make happen is for the organization to reach a point where it effectively leads itself.

Companies are beginning to provide their employees with access to the portal from both work and home. Several companies, such as Ford Motor Company, Delta Airlines, and Dell Computer, provide employees with subsidized computers and Internet access so that they can go online from home. Others simply provide access to employees who already have Internet accounts at home or at remote locations.

In so doing, companies are beginning to reduce the number of environments that employees must manage. New personal devices on the market today now support the type of environment that can provide the richness of a B2E portal. Imagine if you had one identification, one password, and one environment, no matter what device you were using or where you were using it. The concept of *anywhere, anytime* is beginning to evolve. But now it is *my environment—it's about me.*

Almost all of the B2E portals under development offer a personalized home page, which contains some relevant corporate information. This can be in the form of a daily message from the CEO or the latest company news, but the key is that it can be personalized by an individual to include almost any external content they desire. The employee can now include news, weather, sports, banking information, travel, photo albums, investments, e-mail, and calendar. We're even seeing nanny-cams that allow an employee to keep an eye on the day care setting of their child from their portal.

Privacy, of course, remains a paramount issue in this scenario. Employees are likely to be uncomfortable with this melding of their personal and professional lives and will need reassurance from the CEO that a clear boundary remains in place. Companies, for example, will continue to require ownership of e-mail systems, and in a B2E environment, clear codes of conduct must be communicated. Employees who insist on retaining personal e-mail accounts outside the company can have those accounts incorporated into their portals, but away from corporate access.

"Security is critical to constructing rich, interactive relationships with employees, customers, and partners, and enabling them to access and dynamically interact with the vast array of information and applications that resides across the enterprise," said Barry Bycoff, president, chairman, and CEO of Netegrity. "In the automotive industry, suppliers want to access the manufacturer inventory systems which are applicable to their business and allowing them to ship supplies when the inventory is low. In the health care industry, doctors want to access and update patient records, and then share applicable information with the patient's other physicians, health care provider, or pharmacy in order to provide the best care possible. It is about relationships founded on trust. B2E provides a compelling framework for customers to deliver these secure, on-line relationships."

By eliminating that gulf between the personal and professional life, the B2E portal drastically changes all relationships and emotional boundaries between work and home. Once you put this model along with the portal in place, it grows and people want to move real work to the web. It inspires the workforce to the highest levels of performance, not because of some CEO's edict, but because of an inevitable transformation that occurs with the advent of the portal. There is a transition where it is no longer about the company, but about the people themselves. It becomes personal.

How, you might ask, is this achieved? In Chapter 7, "Leadership," you will read about the challenges of leading in a true B2E environment. This is not your father's corporate hierarchy anymore. This is a leadership issue of which many are afraid because most executives want to lead and *manage,* not just lead. Some leaders, like Jacques Nasser at Ford, fall victim to declining economic fortunes before they can complete their B2E missions.

By allowing employees to mostly self-manage their careers within the organization, the portal becomes a tool for increasing loyalty and personal investment in a company at a time when just the opposite is happening across corporate America.

For example, at PwC, we are implementing a B2E portal across our big, diverse firm. For a consulting firm, which has made a massive investment in content, it has long amazed our partners how difficult it is to access needed information as quickly as we'd like. On the road constantly, we find ourselves looking for a certain research report or some pertinent data on a client, only to be slowed down by the lack of access and bandwidth. "Do I have the time and energy to search for that information?" we often ask ourselves.

Our response is to assign the task to someone else who often turns to several others in this quest. So we end up with multiple layers of bureaucracy, which effectively slow rather than quicken the search for information. As we said earlier, this is an incredibly inefficient use of resources. The portal is already changing that scenario, offering faster, better, easier-to-navigate access to people and information across the firm. Partners are able to organize their world—their work lives and their personal lives—in far more efficient ways. By automating such research on the web, we are eliminating unnecessary layers of middle management, cutting overhead staff, and effectively flattening the organization. By connecting everyone to everyone else, we cut down on meetings, but we also create a common corporate culture across all boundaries—geographical and functional—so people feel a part of something bigger than just the people whom they sit next to.

Not only does this new channel make each individual person more effective, but multiply that effectiveness across the firm and you see that the results are tremendous. Perhaps most important, the portal has become the *global glue* that ties the firm together. Not only does it offer everyone direct access to crucial information when and where we need it, but it allows new employees to tap into the corporate wisdom quickly, making them more productive for clients. And finally, as the work gets more and more distributed across the portal, it gets the message and the corporate strategy closer to the customer. This can only be good.

As you will see in the following chapters, getting prepared for B2E is a challenge, but an acceptable challenge if an organization has the will and the kind of leadership that understands the underlying necessity of these changes. Though we are still early in the B2E revolution, the luxury of standing on the sideline and waiting for the pioneers to get the arrows in the back is passing quickly.

CHAPTER TWO
Lessons for B2E

A business book without lessons to take away is not of much value. As you read the following case studies, you will hopefully find a raft of ideas from each one to bring back to your staff. Because each of our case study companies is unique with its own organizational structure, management style, and culture, the implementation and effects of a B2E will vary in impact and scope. When we began our work with HP, for example, the company was in the midst of the economic boom of the late 1990s and faced the future with a new CEO in Carleton S. "Carly" Fiorina. Coming from Lucent with a stellar reputation for leadership in the high-tech sector, she was the first outsider to lead HP. Neither she nor anyone else among the executive staff had any inkling about the magnitude of the coming downturn. But Fiorina did understand that HP's business model could no longer sustain the company's growth heading into the future.

We had no idea that HP would initiate a merger with Compaq Computer, and as we were writing this book, that merger was very much in its early stages. How it would play out, or if it would ever reach fruition, was still unknown. Skeptics appeared in droves immediately after the deal was announced, and Wall Street did not stamp its approval on the merger. However, Fiorina and Michael Capellas, Compaq's CEO, were firm in their resolve to turn the merged company into the second biggest technology company in the world. And the B2E portal would play a significant role in the merger as it unfolded.

Ford Motor Company bears little resemblance to HP. As an old-line manufacturing company, Ford, like its automotive counterparts, seemed like the last place one would find e-business innovation and the embrace of the Internet. Ford made a commitment to B2E that encompasses literally every part of the organization. As the fourth largest company in the United States and one of the largest in the world, Ford's issues with a global implementation of B2E in many ways dwarf what HP is doing. But we also found commonalities across corporate borders.

The same could be said for PricewaterhouseCoopers (PwC). As a giant professional services firm and a partnership, PwC seemingly has little in common with HP or Ford. We don't sell printers, personal computers, or cars. Our product is information, which in many ways makes us the ideal candidate for B2E. Interestingly enough, as we remake our firm around the globe, we are encountering many of the same obstacles as everyone else.

The BBC, like PwC, sells an unusual product line: creativity. Yet this remarkably innovative organization, which was founded in 1922 and has had arguably more influence on television and radio than any other single company in the world, struggles to get itself into the twenty-first century. Its embrace of a new finance portal is dramatically reshaping the way the BBC does its work on the business side, and in so doing, may well have a pro-found influence on the creative side as well.

Nonetheless, as unique as each case study is, we believe there are many lessons to be drawn from them. We found 10 case studies that, we believe, cross all boundaries and deserve special attention.

1. To ensure success, a senior executive must be put in place to oversee the B2E effort.

Pulling together a thousand tribes is daunting enough. Trying to do it by committee is impossible. For any B2E initiative to work, the CEO must appoint an executive to lead the B2E effort. We believe that this B2E chief must report directly to the CEO (and most certainly not to the CIO); otherwise, the effort will never gain the corporate momentum it requires to succeed. In fact, we think this position is so important that it should be a management committee spot in the corporate hierarchy. After all, the B2E portal potentially covers every single process within the company, thus ceding tremendous power for those who maintain it.

Further, the resume of the executive should be heavily laden with business and general management background, along with a deep understanding of the IT infrastructure. But because of the diverse nature of the portal efforts that must be brought together under a single umbrella, we believe the prototype B2E chief comes from within the business ranks, not from IT. For example, Jon Flaxman, corporate controller at HP, was given the assignment of leading the B2E effort. Under his forceful leadership, B2E became a way of doing business at HP.

2. Governance is the top priority to be addressed in any implementation.

Speak to anyone implementing a global B2E portal and they will acknowledge that governance issues takes up two-thirds of their time. Georgina Steinsky-Schwartz, chief HR officer at Bell Canada Enterprises, acknowledges that governance is the single most important issue to address in planning to build the B2E portal. "In a large, diverse organization such as ours, we need to set the ground rules for B2E policy and managing change," Steinsky-Schwartz said. "It's not a one-size-fits-all world. Every company is unique and has to structure its rules to fit its cultural and business needs. This covers issues like privacy, who owns the data, home access, and codes of conduct."

There is often an overlap in the B2E initiative. It requires collaboration and participation of a number of different constituencies, and if a company doesn't get that collaboration, it will end up as a collective of independent, loosely held-together portals. Without proper governance, the efficiencies, synergies, and mind sharing that a true B2E implementation offers can never be realized.

As more companies become multinational in scope, governance becomes even more crucial to the portal success. Company-wide projects require tremendous sharing and leveraging across many channels. Such sharing means giving up a certain amount of control, which is anathema to most managers. Managers who can no longer take full credit for success are not usually happy, but the ability to leverage corporate wisdom as never before more than makes up for personal career dilemmas. The only way to ensure the full value of the portal is to incorporate clear and strict governance.

3. In embracing B2E, everybody becomes a media company.

Because the essence of the portal is content, a company in essence becomes a de facto publishing empire made up of dozens of local newspapers or magazines. Though a B2E chief serves as editor, as in any large media company, individual managers or editors will decide on the content. Each has significant freedom to implement an application that suits the needs of their users.

Because of this, companies cannot underestimate the need for communications about the portal. Getting people on board is like selling newspaper subscriptions or advertising. The power of the portal, like a publication, increases exponentially as its user base increases.

"Once we provide people with a single repository for knowledge and information that they see as theirs and use regularly, we'll begin to see people and their enterprises connecting and driving better performance and alignment. Then we'll see huge leaps in productivity and creativity. B2E provides employers with a way of getting there," says Tod Loofburrow, CEO of Authoria, a leading knowledge application company.

4. Navigating the enterprise portal must be intuitive to all employees from the outset.

The portal is personal, therefore it must be designed by employees for use by employees. The look and feel must be easy to embrace and navigate or it will simply not be used. Some of the most ambitious portal efforts we've seen have failed or have been slow to catch on because they were not intuitive. Avoid technical language and remember that the whole notion of anytime, anywhere access is only as good as the system is inviting. "You can't rely on training and thick manuals to get people to use the portal because they won't use those things," said W. James Fish, retired executive director with the Ford Motor Company. "It has to be right from the outset or people will never come back."

5. The CEO and his or her top executives must lead differently in this new environment.

You will read more about leadership in Chapter 7. But CEOs must be aware that to run a company that is B2E-enabled, one must lead differently. You can no longer be the magical voice behind the curtain. The Wizard-of-Oz era is over. With a huge direct channel to everyone in the company, a CEO must be out front and visible. Under this new environment, it is about being authentic and being transparent. As you will read, management can and should use the B2E portal to establish a new relationship with employees. At Ford, Jacques Nasser initiated with all employees a weekly, online dialogue called "Let's Chat," a seemingly small gesture that has had an enormous impact on the company's employees.

6. Management has to understand the implications of this potent new communications channel.

Because of its power and ubiquity, the portal is likely to change people's lives, not just at work, but at home as well. Every step in communications over the course of history has changed the world. So the implications of the Internet and this new channel are probably bigger than most of us can imagine today. This is no longer just about work, and therefore the very notion of managing in this environment requires a new way to think about the relationships networking throughout the organization. It may be some time before all the implications of this new channel become clear, especially in a global organization.

"The B2E portal will allow us to communicate and

share our business metrics and results with every employee on a real-time basis," said Klaus Kleinfeld, CEO of Siemens Corporation. "This information should empower our employees to achieve our business goals more precisely. In this way, the portal will connect people to each other, to their business units, and to the company in ways that were never possible before. This alignment will produce better business results."

7. Though the rewards are great, a B2E implementation is a long journey.

Over and over again, we've seen companies underestimate the difficulties and obstacles associated with a portal implementation. Despite the fact that the organization does not have to tear out entrenched systems and build expensive new ones, a B2E implementation is not as intuitive and straightforward as one might think. After all, this is about changing the way people work and think. It is about transforming corporate hierarchies and dramatically impacting corporate cultures. Anyone who promises that this is easy is guilty of gross oversimplification.

"In a traditional systems implementation, there is usually a two-year effort to design, develop, and implement the system before it reaches production and people actually use it," said Sam Berger, a PwC Consulting partner. "In a B2E implementation a portal can be built in three to four months, but that is only the beginning. Once a new reality is created, the opportunity to change behavior and reap rewards begins."

8. B2E is NOT about technology.

Most major technology initiatives over the past decade, whether they were traditional technology implementation or the embrace of e-business, have fallen prey to the IT mentality within an organization. The initiative becomes a *project* (often seen by employees as a program du jour) and becomes mired in techno-speak and the IT bureaucracy. B2E is about transforming the organization by moving work to the web. It is about changing the relationship between the employee and the work and changing the very work processes themselves.

"Our big 'aha' is that this is not a technology problem," said David Erickson, Pfizer's vice president of HR shared services. "It is an issue about global service delivery models and governance."

In fact, if the portal is not transparent and easy to use, it will die under its own weight. We've seen many portal implementations struggle because of technology, and most often, it is the underlying systems already in place, not the portal, that slows the process.

9. *The CEO must champion the B2E effort.*

Though a B2E chief is essential, B2E itself will go nowhere unless the CEO gets visibly, vocally, and emotionally behind the effort. After all, this is transformative and cannot be handed off to others like marketing or finance. Every successful B2E implementation we've seen has been championed by the CEO. The vision must come from the CEO, and he or she must lead it, publicly and privately.

"CEOs play different roles in organizations—some are visionaries, some are leaders, others manage—but regardless of their roles, business transformation cannot succeed without the clear leadership of the CEO. The leadership of the CEO is critical to the success of the transformational aspects of B2E," says Craig Conway, CEO of PeopleSoft.

10. There will be a network effect: The multiplication of intelligence will indeed create corporate wisdom.

We have observed over and over again what is known as the *network effect* when B2E implementations get momentum. The network effect produces a multiplication of intelligence throughout the organization, thus increasing corporate wisdom on a global basis. By creating virtual teams around the globe, an economist in New York can work closely with his or her counterpart in New Delhi on a real-time basis. These teams working in this environment are likely to produce endless opportunities for creativity and profit.

"We're at a new juncture in technology," says Gordon Eubanks, a veteran Silicon Valley entrepreneur and currently CEO of Oblix. "We spent the last twenty-five years focused on the relationship between an individual and technology in building better devices, networks, personal productivity tools, and business applications. Now we're moving into a new era in which our focus is on connecting people to each other and reaping those benefits."

GETTING TO A THOUSAND POINTS OF LIGHT
Apologies to the senior George Bush, but we believe that a well-crafted, strategically implemented B2E portal can transform a company from a thousand tribes into thousands of points of communication, collaboration, and creativity.

As you read on, you will see in our case study companies the power of B2E to turn autonomy and disconnection into community, by moving work to the web and transforming the way people work. As we said at the beginning of this chapter, business is nothing if it is not cyclical. Our case study companies may be mired in calamitous economic woes or on the verge of tremendous promise. We cannot predict these short-term cycles any more than famed economists and futurists.

What we can say is that the commitment to B2E is a long-term one with the potential for significant cost reductions, improved productivity, and the transformation of the way people work. The epiphany is that there is indeed a means to harness the power of the Internet and bring together organizations in this new, unprecedented way. The good news is that it is still early in the game, and the winners are yet to be determined. Wherever you are in your B2E efforts—at the starting gate or well into a big implementation—we hope these cases will be invaluable and inspiring to you as you go forward.

CHAPTER THREE
Hewlett-Packard

In July 1999, when Carleton S. "Carly" Fiorina became chairman and chief executive of Hewlett-Packard (HP) Company, she inherited an American industry icon with fraying edges. The then $42 billion technology giant had long been considered among the world's corporate elite with its ceaseless commitment to product innovation, marketing excellence, and employee satisfaction. Hewlett-Packard has been a perennial choice for "Most Admired Companies" and "Best Places to Work" lists and a Wall Street darling for much of its 64-year existence. The "HP Way," the widely admired corporate Zeitgeist created by founders William Hewlett and David Packard, had become the stuff of books and business folklore.

But in the ever-shifting sine waves of business, even the best-run corporations stumble. And the HP that Fiorina encountered had become that classic business cliché: a victim of its own success. Years of double-digit growth coupled with the largely autonomous work environment had created a bloated, heavily decentralized, unmanageable giant.

Fiorina discovered, for example, that HP had been run as a holding company—much like General Electric—with an astounding 83 product lines, each operating as a self-directed business unit. In essence, each of these businesses had its own general manager making his or her decisions and an infrastructure designed in silolike fashion to service that particular business. Hewlett-Packard's 90,000 employees, scattered around 127 countries, had drifted further and further beyond the echoes of communications from the corporate center.

"When I came here, I described HP as a company of a thousand tribes," Fiorina says. "We had more than one thousand internal web sites for employee training, for example. There were more than three thousand intranets delivering some form of human resource information. What happened over time was that everybody rolled their own. Everybody went off and did their own thing on everything."

Thousands of web sites and applications were thrown up on the Internet with the mistaken notion that if content and services were put on an intranet, employees would discover them and use them. Among such intranets were sites for travel reservations, room scheduling, corporate communications, product information, marketing, sales-force automation, product configuration, and pricing. In truth, few found these sites and even fewer used them.

The other result was that employees did not know which web sites to use or whether the ones they chose had complete and up-to-date information. Without a single authoritative data source, employees wasted significant time searching for information. In other words, they missed a lot, often not knowing what they didn't know. All of this resulted in frustration and low productivity.

Communications, the watchword of a new-millennium company, had become stymied at every turn. "It was very difficult to reach all employees on a consistent basis," Fiorina says. "I'd send a message out and I didn't know who got it. I didn't know who heard it. I didn't know who reacted to it." Ironically, in a company devoted to solving customers' technology dilemmas, HP was caught in the classic corporate bind. "I'm working for technology," Fiorina would point out in frustration. "Technology isn't working for me."

Clearly, what had worked for six decades was no longer going to suffice at HP. The HP Way was built upon an unusual but dynamic premise: "Give me autonomy. Give me the resources. Give me the capabilities and I'll prove that I can do great things," HP managers were taught to believe. "Show me how I'm going to be measured and I'll tell you how I'll behave."

Indeed, in 1997, HP initiated an independent assessment of its culture, and a survey of the top 300 senior managers showed a corporate culture that was "four sigma" from the norm in terms of autonomy. In other words, HP managers had far more autonomy than their counterparts at the average corporation, says Steven J. Rice, director of HP's Human Resources Global Enterprise Programs and Technology. "We were literally off the scale in the sense of how much autonomy was part of our culture, part of our corporate DNA."

For Fiorina, the need for a dramatic overhaul of HP seemed obvious. "Our interactions with employees mirrored our organizational structure," she says. "This was a product company organized around product lines. So over time, we had devolved into an exceptionally decentralized structure which had become—with the growing size and complexity of the company—very redundant, very inefficient, and very confusing to employees."

Coupled with HP's internal infrastructure problems was the dramatically shifting business landscape. In the summer of 2001, Fiorina orchestrated a merger with Compaq Computer Corporation. The bold announcement would turn the two companies into a single, giant $80 billion corporation with 145,000 employees, the second largest in the computer industry, and a competitor for IBM. At the time of publication, the deal was awaiting stockholder and regulatory approval.

Whatever the outcome, implementing a new corporate strategy without clear and widespread channels of communication is daunting. How do you ensure that the right messages have been heard? How do you get managers and employees involved in the change when you have to rely on an uncommitted layer of middle management? The portal plays a significant role in addressing those questions.

Regardless of what happens with the merger, those same communications issues haunted HP before the deal was proposed. If employees were confused, so too were customers and suppliers. Product development in key markets such as high-end servers and data storage had failed to generate the desired results to fuel growth. Hewlett-Packard's vaunted brand name remained strong, but Fiorina was not content to risk letting the company rest on its laurels. Compounding the situation was the timing of her arrival.

Fiorina had landed in the midst of the dot-com hysteria, which had swept Wall Street, the venture capital community, and the entire high-tech sector. The Internet had begun to change everything, for big and small companies alike, and executives were scrambling to carve out a blueprint for the near-term and long-term future. While Fiorina never bought into the hype and hysteria, she believed that something fundamental was happening and that the Internet and e-services would become the foundation for the future of business. Hewlett-Packard seemed well positioned to become an e-services powerhouse if Fiorina could capture the moment and push through dramatic change.

MOVING TOWARD REINVENTION

Fiorina knew she needed to transform the company—not only how work was done, but the work itself. She moved swiftly. During the first months of her tenure, she began to institute a sweeping reinvention of HP and how it does business. To frame her vision and unite the thousand tribes, Fiorina unveiled "The Rules of the Garage" to all employees. Referencing HP's humble beginnings in 1938 in a Palo Alto garage, Fiorina laid out her mandate to the company:

→ Believe you can change the world.

→ Work quickly, keep the tools unlocked, work whenever.

→ Share tools, ideas.

→ Trust your colleagues.

→ No politics.

→ No bureaucracy. (These are ridiculous in a garage.)

→ The customer defines a job well done.

→ Radical ideas are not bad ideas.

→ Invent different ways of working.

→ Make a contribution every day. If it doesn't contribute, it doesn't leave the garage.

➜ Believe that together we can do anything.

➜ Invent.

In difficult economic times, corporate edicts and mission statements often get trampled in the rush to the exits. For Fiorina, however, the Rules of the Garage were embodied in the sweeping changes that she set forth at HP. Her idea was to reignite the company's passion for creativity, product leadership, collaboration, customer satisfaction, and an intolerance for corporate bureaucracy. What would be eliminated was the sprawling network of fiefdoms that HP had become.

The 83 autonomous business units were pared down to 17. Before Fiorina had arrived, HP had approved the spin-off of a significant part of its test and medical devices business into a separate company called Agilent Technologies. But she inherited the task of overseeing the breakup, which meant shifting more than 30,000 employees to a brand new enterprise. At the same time, she took the remainder of HP and shaped it into four vast organizations and dramatically altered 64 years of corporate history. She and the executive council issued an edict: Overall infrastructure costs needed to be reduced by $1 billion. No longer would every product line have its own business organization. The new HP would become a *front-end/back-end* organizational structure.

Under the new structure, one back-end unit develops and builds computers. Another builds imaging equipment and printers. The product units work in collaboration with two front-end sales and marketing units to refine and develop new products. One sells to consumers, the other to corporate customers. According to *Business Week* magazine, the new structure is intended to "boost collaboration, giving sales and marketing execs a direct pipeline to engineers so products are developed from the ground up to solve customer problems."[1] The magazine called the plan "so radical that experts say it has never been tried before at a company of HP's size and complexity."

Attempting to remake a giant company in the midst of an economic downturn is always fraught with peril. Chief executives must keep a strong hand on the tiller as quarterly results are carefully scrutinized by the financial markets, but they also must steer through treacherous rapids toward their future vision. Cost cutting, layoffs, stock price erosion, and an endless list of unexpected challenges combine to make such reinvention that much more difficult at tradition-bound companies like HP. Despite this, Fiorina was confident in her plan. At a talk with employees, Fiorina said, "We looked in the mirror and saw a great company that was becoming a failure. This is the vision Bill and Dave, the company's founders, would have had if they were sitting here today."

For Fiorina, a crucial element of her strategy emerged from an unexpected but key sector of the company: human resources. It was there that the modest beginnings of HP's B2E initiative began in December 1999 and later evolved into the company's new central nervous system, the enterprise portal called @*hp*.

While most large companies have begun to embrace the portal concept, HP's effort to build a corporate-wide online channel is well ahead of the pack. Fiorina immediately recognized the potential of @hp, not only as an example of deploying e-services inside the company, but for its role as an integrating mechanism, the catalyst for change, that would help her put into operation the new front-end/back-end model. Such an organizational structure would require unprecedented levels of collaboration.

Fiorina didn't come upon her B2E views by chance. She had closely studied the highly regarded model put in place at Silicon Valley neighbor Cisco Systems. As a member of Cisco's board of directors, Fiorina had a firsthand glimpse of the way that Cisco had leveraged the Internet to remake its business model and gain industry-shaking competitive advantage. Part of Cisco's success came from allowing customers to place orders online and the integration of all of the processes that led to the delivery of those orders. Fiorina recognized the value of this but considered it a beginning to even more ambitious plans for the web.

While most companies were drawing portal plans, HP's portal was already winning awards for its breadth and scope and drawing attention to the massive effort. Though it remains a work in progress—in many ways a living corporate organism that will grow and extend its reach over several years—@hp has been at the heart of the company's transformation and will grow in importance over time.

What began as an HR portal for employees is now well beyond that, Fiorina says. As each corporate function (e.g., finance, purchasing, marketing, engineering, and operations) moves to the portal, it will expand its role well beyond the walls of HP and become the pulsing connection between work and home for most employees. Further, it is through the same portal that HP will connect to customers, suppliers, and business partners, thus making it the company's de facto central nervous system. "The portal is the connecting point for the essence of the process reinvention we're now going through," Fiorina says.

Her goals are ambitious. She envisions a time in which 95 percent of all work at HP will be done through the @hp portal. For example, HP sales reps can access the portal to obtain up-to-date and comprehensive information about product releases. At the same time, HP's reinvention will mean moving away from disparate, inconsistent, conflicting, and incomplete processes, web sites, databases, and information sets to a world of consistent and complete shared processes, information, and databases. "It forces a rigor," she says. "It raises the bar for all business managers."

Indeed, HP is a stellar example of how B2E is becoming *the* catalyst for business transformation, evolving from business to employee into the far more powerful concept of business to *everything*.

PORTAL BEGINNINGS

Steven Rice, who has led HP's portal effort since its inception, began the initial project in late 1998 when Susan Bowick, HP's vice president for HR, asked him to investigate the feasibility of moving a significant amount of the company's global HR transaction capabilities to the HP web site. The transactions included employee data (e.g., change of address, benefits administration, stock holdings, and retirement plans), all tied to the company's policy information. The week Rice finished his investigation, however, the company decided to split the company in two and create Agilent Technologies. Rice's project was immediately shelved because of the huge investment in time and resources the spin-off would entail.

When Fiorina joined HP in mid-1999, she had ordered a benchmark study done comparing HP's infrastructure to those at other well-managed companies. When the results came back, Fiorina knew she needed a dramatic change. She and the executive council announced their plan to reduce overall infrastructure costs by $1 billion. In mid-October 1999, each of the global function leaders was given six weeks to identify his or her strategies to meet the new cost goals established by the benchmarking study.

What Bowick unearthed during her deep examination of the HR organization was sobering. Hewlett-Packard's

HR organization was suffering from the effects of high cost, low customer satisfaction, and an inability to add real value to the business. She discovered excessively complex processes, technology systems that were not integrated, and an overly complex organizational structure in effect consisting of a completely separate and self-supporting HR organization for each business. Indeed, though earlier attempts had been made at shared services and web delivery, the HR organization continued to breed a complex and customized environment. This led to expensive reward programs, confusing variations in key processes like staffing, and literally hundreds of custom-made web sites posted without any concern about a cohesive and coordinated effort.

Beyond the growing confusion, the complexity was expensive. In 1999, for example, HP's HR costs were $3,200 per employee compared with $2,365 per employee in competing companies. In addition, HP's autonomous culture had undermined the many efforts at creating coordinated call centers and web sites that would provide timely, accurate information to HP employees around the country and the world. With everybody doing their own thing, web-based applications were not well organized. Processes relied on paper forms and labor-intensive data input. Back-office technologies were agonizingly uncoordinated and fragmented.

In a company trying to sell seamless technology solutions to its customers, HP's culture turned its employees into the classic cobbler's children. In this case, they did without, not because of the lack of technology, but because of the lack of corporate cohesion and synergy. Exceptions had become the norm. Every function, business, and country had its own set of web sites with customized tools and information.

Employees relied on the face-to-face, high-touch experience—indeed, this was the essence of the HP Way—but as the company grew, the demands outstripped the system's capacity to handle them. Human resources staffs ballooned to unwieldy numbers. Processes bogged down. Benefits guidelines, for example, had to be updated manually each year and placed in thick three-ring binders. Administrators had to spend countless hours updating the paper-based systems and always seemed to be a day behind.

The result was low customer satisfaction with the HR function. Human resources was simply not delivering what managers valued. A survey of the company's general managers revealed that they were not getting the kind of highly valued services they needed (e.g., competitive compensation, recruiting, and change management support).

For Bowick, the challenge of remaking the HR function was doubled by Fiorina's fiat to reduce costs. Human resources costs needed to be cut by a whopping 20 percent. She and Rice decided that one of the most effective ways to cut costs would be to revive Rice's former project and move significant work to an HR web site. A well-designed and executed web site could reduce administrative costs in the call centers, reduce transaction-processing time, and increase value to employees. In December 1999, HP signed an agreement with PricewaterhouseCoopers (PwC), the giant accounting and consulting firm, to help build the HR web site. From the outset, the plan was to produce a corporate portal, not simply another web site to add to HP's vast collection.

As usually happens with such dynamic projects, the portal work set off a tidal wave of other project proposals, in effect triggering a complete organizational transformation, from the technology back-end to the front-end connection to the employee population. "We quickly saw that the larger prize would be to elevate this to something that the entire enterprise could utilize," Rice says. "We believed this was something other internal infrastructure organizations could use to address their own similar issues to HR: cutting costs, creating value."

As often happens, corporate politics intervened and the project almost died before getting off the ground. At a meeting in Geneva in February 2000, the PwC team was informed that the plug might be pulled. Though Bowick was solidly behind the effort, other executives in HP's HR hierarchy had serious doubts about spending the $15 million to $20 million to build the portal. "If the company is trying to save money, why spend this kind of money on something untested and unknown?" they asked.

It was Fiorina herself who ended the debate. It was time for HP to become one company with a streamlined structure optimized for the new millennium. Fiorina understood that a B2E effort is doomed to failure if the CEO is not firmly on board and actively and visibly leading the charge. In the second week of February, Fiorina sent out a directive to the entire company announcing the HR portal and its importance for the company. If HP was going to be a leading e-services company, it had to bring its e-services capabilities inside and make them tangible and real for its 90,000 employees. She nicknamed the effort "Project Mighty Dog," in effect telling the employees it was "time to start eating our own dog food."

TO HR AND BEYOND

As the portal effort ramped up, two things quickly became clear: The portal would become nothing less than the fulcrum for the reinvention of the company, and HR would be the first function on the portal but certainly not the last. Over a multiyear period, all of the company's functional areas, from finance to purchasing to marketing to engineering, as well as critical business processes, such as sales and marketing tools, and new product development, would migrate to the portal. However, implementing the portal and making it work would be a massive challenge, perhaps the toughest task anyone at HP had ever undertaken. It required a corporate gut check because it is an excruciatingly painful process—an open-ended, demanding journey rather than a self-contained, one-off project.

The HP and PwC team soon realized that three critical elements must be addressed immediately and effectively in order for the effort to have a chance to succeed:

1. Governance
2. Content and services
3. Technology

What companies such as HP are learning as they embrace B2E is that in order for the effort to succeed, they must set up a clear and understandable framework for tackling the business issues surrounding the portal. Corporate standards addressing access, privacy, security, and a whole raft of similar issues must be considered and put firmly and quickly in place. "By the nature of the Internet, you can't have ten different processes that you move to a solution like this," Bowick says. "You have to have governance that sticks and do it quickly so that you can move in Internet time." That's not all. Behavioral changes—getting everyone to do things the same way—and role changes must accompany the portal implementation. Countless jobs changed either a little or a lot, depending on their proximity to processes that were reengineered for @hp. For example, content management has become something that nearly everyone has to do.

And every manager has to do salary planning and performance evaluations online.

In addition, a corporate B2E chief must be put in charge of the effort so it doesn't flounder or sink under the weight of too many cooks. Without governance, the effort will simply morph back into an online version of the corporate chaos that existed before.

The second piece of the puzzle involves moving work to the web. Deciding what content and services will be moved and, simultaneously, deciding how to transform the organization to adapt to these changes are key. Moving work to the web without changing the way people are organized to do that work will yield diminished or negative results. "You have to have some process in program management that spans multiple organizations and can get things rolling," Bowick says. "This is not an ad hoc situation, 'Here's a good idea, let's slap it on the portal.' There has to be rigor that goes around managing this as a serious business asset."

And addressing the technology issues is an especially complex but critical piece of the puzzle. Hewlett-Packard rounded up all its major technology partners and brought them inside to tackle the massive internal effort. But corralling a vast, decentralized technological environment such as HP's is no easy task. And building a robust, seamless, debugged network around a giant global corporation is daunting. Companies that simply toss the portal effort over the wall to the CIO and the IT organization will likely fail. In fact, all three elements must be addressed in a coordinated effort.

The technology piece is certainly crucial and challenging. The HP and PwC team spent the first six months working on a portal engine developed by outside vendors. Just three months before the portal was to be launched, the team discovered that the engine would not work properly due to its complexity in passing data back and forth through the company firewall. Fiorina had announced that the portal would go live in the summer and now that deadline was in jeopardy.

The team was nearly frantic—"We've built the car but the engine doesn't work," they thought. But being in a technology center like HP in the heart of the Silicon Valley, there was no shortage of engineers who loved a challenge. A core team of HP and PwC people worked with a small start-up named Epicentric and built a new engine in 60 days. The portal was up and running close to Fiorina's deadline.

However, creating the technology piece alone is not enough. Nowhere has that been more evident than at HP. Fiorina understood from the outset that the B2E effort would start out modestly as a way to automate existing processes and evolve into something much greater. She compared the B2E effort with the business-to-business (B2B) revolution. "B2B evolved into e-marketplaces that fundamentally changed the nature of relationships between companies and suppliers," she says. "It is a way to build ecosystems and perfect markets, and I believe the same thing will happen with B2E over time."

Fiorina believes that HP's experience is a template for other companies. Human resources is an obvious starting point for most companies implementing portals. An HR portal can quickly transform and impact the company's connection to its employees and ramp up their productivity.

For example, a single password allows HP managers access to current data on their worldwide workforce: attrition, organizational structure, diversity, hiring, and administration of salary and stock programs including access to collaboration tools to enable employees from everywhere around the globe to work together on a virtual basis. Net meeting provides a virtual forum to share documents during real-time discussions—reducing the need for time-wasting and exhausting travel. Document management tools with check-in and check-out facilities ensure security and version control, allowing one region to move a work product forward while people in another region are sleeping. Active web site management and convergence on the portal eliminates hours of frustrating and fruitless search for information.

Above all, having these tools accessible through a single portal window means that a lot more people use them. Hewlett-Packard had online procurement for office supplies and online travel before the portal was built, for example, but no one could remember the URL addresses. Traffic on the sites was dismal. Now that these same applications are available and easy to find through @hp, traffic has skyrocketed. Additional savings from the link to our procurement system, Ariba, are estimated at $50 million annually.

DOUBLE-DOWN

Along the way, the HP and PwC Consulting team have learned many hard lessons. Foremost is that employees care little about the origins of a problem; they just want to get their work done. They want to connect with each other without worrying about silos and organizational boundaries. Territorial boundaries between functions are insignificant to individuals, and what executives might view as an HR problem or a finance problem or an operations procurement problem blur together for employees. As Rice points out, "If you talk to employees, they will say, 'That's great. You solved *your* problem, but it doesn't solve my problem as an employee or manager.' "

Thus, a blending of ideas and implementations is crucial . . . along with an indelible commitment to stay the course. As Fiorina soon learned, the initial burst of enthusiasm for the portal was followed rapidly by a wave of despair. "When you get into the really tough stuff, people start saying, 'Oh my God, this is much harder than I thought, therefore it's not going to work,' " she explains. "People fall by the wayside and many companies give up way too soon."

In spite of some internal soul-searching, Fiorina knew the project needed to proceed. "We had to go through a period when we thought, 'Do we bag @hp because it's harder than we thought, or do we double-down and put everything into it and say we're going to take the time to make it work?" she says. "The only way to deal with cynicism over time is to prove people wrong. The only way to prove people wrong is to keep at it. Beyond that, we had to tell people that once it works, we're going to use it as a centerpoint and a fulcrum for many other business process reinventions we have to do. We've made that latter choice and it's the right choice."

To reinforce the magnitude of the decision, Fiorina and Bowick agreed to a dramatic opening. On the day the portal went live, HP unplugged major organizations and support services within HR to coerce people into using the portal. For example, the only way to partake in open enrollment for all benefits in the United States was to log on to the portal. That got 46,000 employees on the portal the day it went live.

Nonetheless, Fiorina had to endure a period when e-mails and phone calls poured in. Hewlett-Packard's face-to-face culture had thrived for more than a half-century, and, though nearly all employees understood the need for dramatic changes, the impact and the reality of that change hit hard. "It's not like it used to be!" people wailed. "It doesn't work." Hewlett-Packard's employees weren't afraid of a challenge. Indeed, HP has long been noted for its highly motivated and loyal workforce. But in the face of deep cutbacks, layoffs, the splitting off of Agilent, and a bleak economy, the arrival of the portal left many feeling like strangers in a strange land.

For HP workers, the pain was centered on the extreme complexities of the implementation of the portal. Creating a stable, robust internal global network to service 90,000 employees in 127 countries in multiple languages was a huge challenge. It was fraught with technological and cultural landmines, and HP had no map or blueprint to lead the way.

Thus, there were fears mixed with tremendous expectations and a range of perceptions about what would transpire. Once Fiorina decided to go down that road, she said, "This is it. This is the doorway through which our employees are going to access all the tools and information they need to be productive and valued in their jobs. There aren't any choices now. We've invested in @hp and this is where you've got to go."

Among the early perceptions was that the portal was switched on and previous business practices shut down before the portal was ready to handle the load. One 23-year HP veteran said the result was near chaos in the HR function. Groups had been cut drastically in anticipation of work being shifted to the Internet and the portal. The face-to-face contact with an HR representative, which had been a de facto entitlement for employees, was gone almost overnight. Confused employees didn't know how to get basic personnel questions answered. Those who remained in the HR function were buried under an avalanche of work that had once been handled by an army of coworkers, now departed. The U.S. Employee Services Call Center, for example, was cut from 100 to 30 workers when the portal was launched.

"People were working unbelievable hours, weekends, late at night," the manager said. "There was major league stress and a lot of tears of anger and frustration. It was awful."

The feeling persisted that those who had not lost their jobs were not being rewarded for retaining their positions but being punished for surviving. The fact that this was playing out in the HR function was particularly stressful to employees who had long been accustomed to gathering all of their personal data from an HR representative in their group. Suddenly, everything was moved to the portal—every type of personnel data from salary information, benefits, retirement funds, vacation status, to leaves of absence for family illness or death in the family. Employees were expected to find what they needed on the portal. But like any new technology, there is a learning curve. Figuring out how to navigate around the portal was daunting for some, and there were few humans left in the chain to answer the questions.

"It rocked us to our core," Rice states. "The only way you are going to get there is to get managers to let go of a lot of things they used to have control over."

In truth, the portal itself was ready to go. What was often at the heart of early technical problems was HP's complex IT infrastructure. If response time on the portal was slow, it was due to the configuration of the company's network servers around the world. There were traffic jams in the internal corporate network. Mistakes were made that had an impact. But what HP learned quickly is that employees don't care where the root of the problem lies. They just want to get what they need when they need it. If the portal lets them down the first few times they attempt to use it, it is difficult to win them over later.

A METHOD TO THE MADNESS

The decision to launch and learn rather than wait for technical perfection, however, was a key part of HP's portal strategy. Indeed, executives understood that in order to move the corporate pendulum at HP, you must do something radical. Almost intentionally, Rice says, they flipped every switch, turned every knob, and pushed every button on the corporate dashboard in the hopes of destabilizing assumptions that had been made for decades inside the company.

"There was a conscious effort to see how much we could get this moving, knowing that some things would go three steps, some would get all the way to completion, others wouldn't work at all," Rice says. "The idea was to get as much activity and movement around the portal as we could to get people to think out of the box around some of the roles they were playing."

As is expected in such a massive reinvention, the rank and file are prone to question the changes and the company's commitment to seeing all the changes through. Fiorina has remained visible and vocal—staying on message, as the cliché goes—that the transformation is not over and will continue to evolve and change. The goal, says Rice, "is to figure out how you get some stamina around surviving a fairly liquid organizational model, given that the competition is not slowing down and waiting for you to figure all this out."

The determination has paid off. Hewlett-Packard surveys its employees and managers regularly each quarter to get feedback on the transformation efforts. In early 2001, employees were asked to create a list of the top 10 initiatives they felt were going well. The portal made the list, giving credence to Fiorina's posture that time will make the portal more and more a crucial and accepted part of the HP environment. Employees also recognized the portal as the most visible and successful symbol of the reinvention.

Rice is in constant contact with employees and managers about the portal, seeking feedback. Though he still hears disagreement about how a certain component of the portal might have been implemented, he no longer hears dissension about the vision and what HP is trying to achieve. People now ask, "How do I get more? When can I expect this or that? How can we get other infrastructure groups to play as aggressive a role as HR did?" "That gives me the idea that we've stumbled onto something that really will have lasting value," Rice says.

In 2001, CMP Media, a leading technology publisher, awarded its top honors to @hp as the "Best Enterprise Information Portal" at its ninth annual RealWare Awards. The breadth and scope of the portal impressed the judges. Hewlett-Packard was judged well ahead of other companies implementing enterprise-wide portals.

Most of HP's 2,000 managers have embraced the portal enthusiastically. They are able to hold meetings with groups or individuals using online conferencing and chat capabilities, cutting down on expensive travel. They can do product reviews or performance appraisals online. They are able to cut costs and upgrade productivity by having employees manage their own personnel data and other key work-related material via the portal.

Significantly, the portal provides the opportunity for employees to embrace and manage their personal lives in ways heretofore impossible. They can access the company and corporate data from home, and they can access needed lifestyle information while at work using the portal rather than sitting on the telephone. The portal content is available in eight languages, 120 countries, 24-7. Indeed, the personalization of work is one of the most valuable assets that the portal provides.

Mary Haywood, Americas talent acquisition manager based in Roseville, California, and a 17-year HP veteran, says she understood the problems people were encountering with the portal early on, but that she never doubted its value. "I was always very positive about the portal because I could see, as a manager, how it could be a really wonderful tool to use." For Haywood, the portal quickly made a dramatic impact on both her personal and professional life.

Like everyone else in HP today, Haywood logs on to the portal every morning and is greeted with the @hp home page featuring company news, a message from Fiorina, and a host of updated information about each of HP's businesses. She uses the portal at home as well to buy or sell stock, track her 401(k), or finish important work with members of her team who are based in other countries and other time zones.

Haywood's unit was cut from 200 employees to 35 in 2000, and she believes the portal has allowed the unit to deliver the same quality service with a significantly smaller staff. "The portal helps facilitate virtual management," Haywood says. "Only four or five members of my team are in Roseville. The rest are all over the country."

As an example, Haywood says that she is able to handle performance evaluations in a faster, more efficient manner online than she did in time-consuming, face-to-face meetings. "I have a college recruiting manager located in the Midwest," she says. "I was able to submit the performance evaluation online. Salary planning was done online. We're communicating this way. And when you think about how expensive business travel is, these tools become imperative. There is almost nothing you can't do through the portal in terms of managing programs and employees."

If salary planning sounds mundane, consider that this is global salary planning for four regions of the world—Asia Pacific, Europe, the Middle East and Africa, and the United States and the Americas (including Canada and Latin America). This was an enormously complex business, which involved four different processes and completely separate computer systems with separate logins for each.

As a long-time HP employee, Haywood acknowledges that the company's extremely personal, face-to-face culture has been dramatically altered. But she believes the portal is the cornerstone in the company's philosophical change and that, despite some resistance from those who miss the high-touch environment, "this way is much more efficient and effective."

Indeed, the underlying power of the portal is that it may well end up being the vehicle for transporting the HP Way and the best of the old culture into the new millennium. Bowick, Rice, and the portal team have spent countless hours considering this issue. "How do we get that same feeling being part of a 90,000-person organization that we used to get 20 years ago when my general manager walked down the hall and shook my hand and thanked me for a job well done; or when we used to have coffee meetings in the cafeteria with every single employee physically in one building?" Rice asked. "How do you replicate that when you're a global company?"

Rice explains that the portal puts managers and employees at the center of the "HP ecosystem." It allows employees to tap into the culture, business, and management practices and therefore gain more reach and access to information, become much more productive and capable in their jobs, as well as this other thing called a *personal life,* than in other multinational companies. In this way, employees walk away feeling that the company really cares about them in a way another company simply can't replicate, Rice says.

Susan Bowick says that as of mid-2001, the HR portal had begun to receive more than 3 million clicks a day with each person staying online an average of 15 to 20 minutes at a time. The portal, which struggled with an 87 percent uptime when it was first launched, is now at nearly 99 percent uptime as the technical glitches have been smoothed over.

Rice acknowledges that a lot of learning has occurred while trying to support a 24-7 portal environment for a company as vast as HP. Moving that level of volume through a multilevel support methodology without losing anyone has provided the kind of real-world training and experience that can't be acquired in books or weekend courses.

Most important to Fiorina, the portal has already achieved a major milestone. "As CEO, the value is that I know there is a connection with employees that is consistent and complete," she declares. When she sends her daily message now, she knows that every HP employee will see it "and that employees aren't confused about how it is they connect up with tools, capabilities, and information that can make their work lives more productive and satisfying. I didn't know that before."

A PATH TO THE OUTSIDE WORLD

Fiorina's commitment to the portal and B2E does not stop at the boundaries of HP. She has always perceived the portal as a powerful arm to reach out to customers as well. She calls the portal "a perfect example of what we call an intersection of opportunity." The portal illustrates how business process transformation and information technology implementation can come together. Indeed, as the portal has grown in scope, it becomes a remarkably effective marketing tool for the reinvented HP to win over customers who are thinking about e-services and B2E implementations themselves.

"This shows that we are about more than boxes," Fiorina says. To customers, HP has become a true e-services company eating its own dog food. Through the harsh trials and tribulations of the portal experience, HP has learned firsthand about tying together business process understanding with an Internet infrastructure to really transform a relationship.

For example, HP has used the portal to transform a program for finding external temporary workers. Using the portal and a software product called Chimes, which HP purchased from an outside vendor, HP managers can go to the Internet, enter the requirements their business unit has for temporary workers, and those requirements are offered online to a number of temporary agencies (e.g., Manpower, CDI, and Kelley). These agencies can access these requests and provide needed workers quickly.

Mary Haywood, who is overseeing the Chimes effort, says the "time to place,"—getting temps hired and at their desks—the key measure for the effectiveness in finding temp workers, has been cut by 50 percent. Getting workers in place faster and more effectively offers a huge increase in productivity, Haywood says, and the portal makes the entire program possible.

LESSONS

For HP, the portal experience will do nothing less than redefine its business model internally and provide a crucial platform for helping customers embrace a similar model themselves. In essence, HP is experiencing the pain of its own transformation in order to ease the burden for customers who seek the same transformation. Bowick says that customers who adopt what HP has done can personalize it for their own businesses and see a significant return in 9 to 12 months.

Having learned from its own experience, HP can help customers avoid the technology crises that usually accompany massive B2E implementations. "Instead of dealing with the technology, they can spend their energy thinking about how to take advantage of the technology and make changes to get those advantages," she says. "High-tech companies are their own worst enemies because we fall in love with the technology."

Companies opting to follow HP down the B2E path must consider some important lessons, HP executives say. Never underestimate the transformational nature of what you are creating, Rice says. "You are fundamentally changing the way your employees are delivering products and services. The skills and capabilities necessary to provide those services in this way are very different. Getting people ready and able to handle these changes is not an insignificant task."

Fiorina's devotion to the plan is also critical. The portal effort must have executive sponsorship—someone out front, leading the vision, keeping it alive both in the short term and an ongoing basis. "You can't underestimate the importance of that leadership," Rice says.

In @hp, Fiorina sees a microcosm for what it takes to drive behavioral and cultural change. She suggests that executives who opt for a portal as the heart of their B2E effort need to consider three key things: (1) clarity, (2) consistency, and (3) frequency. "You need clarity about where you are going and consistency about the fact that you are going there," Fiorina says. "You have to make it clear, 'We're going to build a portal, and yes we know it's tough and there are problems, but we're going and so are you.' It requires a decision that gets reinforced over and over again."

Along the way, she says, you must incite people, force people to go, and reward people for going; make clear the consequences for not going. "The reason the HP reinvention story is out there is because we burned the boats," Fiorina declares.

The HP portal is expected to be the catalyst for more than *$1 billion in cost savings,* according to Fiorina, and she predicts those savings will increase to several billion dollars over the next few years. However, it's not only about cost savings. For Fiorina, the portal has done nothing less than usher in a new era in business. If the HP-Compaq union becomes a reality, the portal will represent nothing less than the central nervous system of this massive combined entity.

"The Internet is now becoming transformational," she says. "We've finished the end of the beginning and we're now moving into the second phase. But that transformational opportunity is incredibly difficult. What makes it difficult is not the technology, which can be fixed pretty easily. What makes it difficult is the people and their method of operation, their governance, how they interact, the discipline that is required, and how all of that has to change. And more often than not, that's why people give up. People have to change how they work in fundamental ways, and it is very hard."

The power of B2E in the next phase of its implementation is how much power it actually bestows on the individual, she says. When the portal is fully implemented and firing on all cylinders, it will result in technology truly working for the individual for the first time. Employees will have access to information, make choices, find tools that allow technology to work for them in vastly different ways than in the past. "Technology is most powerful when it disappears; when it becomes pervasive, invisible, and so intuitive that you don't think of the technology at all," Fiorina says.

If Fiorina gets her wish, HP will emerge from its transformation with a simple message for its employees and customers: *HP is a winning e-company with a shining soul.* "We are saying that in the markets in which we choose to compete, we're playing to win," Fiorina says. "We're a company that's known for understanding, leveraging, and capitalizing on its e-enabling capabilities. But we're also a company that continues to be known as much for its strength of character as for the strength of its results."

CHAPTER FOUR

Ford Motor Company

n 1996, with the advent of the web and successful online efforts by the likes of America Online (AOL) and Amazon.com, the early seeds of B2E got underway at Ford Motor Company. Though it may seem mundane today, at the time, Ford's efforts were dramatic, especially for a traditional corporation of its size and scope.

One key online initiative began in the Ford HR department under W. James Fish, who was then executive director of HR operations. Fish, along with David W. Cooper, director of HR information and systems planning, brought together a small group of Ford managers and outside consultants to figure out how to drive the transformation of HR. The objective: Reengineer the basic business processes within HR so that the group was better aligned with the business objectives of the company. "We wanted to anticipate and lead change for Ford as opposed to being reactive," Fish says. "We also wanted to improve the overall quality of our services, shorten our cycle time for delivery, and most importantly, reduce costs."

Despite the lack of enterprise portal software that exists today from vendors like SAP Portals, Epicentric, and PeopleSoft, the planners decided that an enterprise portal was the correct solution. Building such a portal with internal software tools would be a difficult and time-consuming job, but if such a corporate-wide system could be deployed, it would be a powerful tool. Before the now-hackneyed term *disintermediation* was even uttered, Ford began disintermediating the HR function. At a company as large as Ford, with 350,000 employees in 160 countries, the very idea of such access to personal information and Ford's HR policies was a persuasive motivator for the team.

Though the Internet was just beginning to emerge as a tool for this effort, Fish's team viewed self-service as the key to the makeover. If a Ford worker in the Kansas City assembly plant had a question about benefits or leaves of absence in the pre-Internet environment, he or she had to go to an HR representative to find the answer. Some issues might be simple and straightforward. Others might require layers of people and bureaucracy to find the correct answer. All this took considerable time and money. But what if that employee could avoid having to interface with an HR representative and go to the service center directly? Wouldn't he or she get better information directly and close the loop more quickly?

The drive to self-service became the mantra and as two years passed, the idea of an Internet-based HR portal began to materialize. If an online portal could be implemented throughout the company, around the globe, it could eventually tie Ford together in ways heretofore unthinkable.

For a company with a century of organizational history, the bureaucratic pilings have been driven deep into the firmament. Ford had always been run by countries, functions, and brands. Different business rules existed for different functions. In Germany, for example, the Jaguar division had its own product development and manufacturing processes, its own administrative processes and rules, and different HR people for each of those units. If Ford could somehow centralize, standardize, and reengineer those core processes, it would offer a potent competitive edge. A portal, Fish's group realized, could be the answer.

Funding for the HR portal came in January 1998. Fish's group benchmarked other companies to find a basis for comparison with Ford's internal processes. Like other companies in the burgeoning Internet age, there was a veritable cornucopia of policies and information systems bringing HR to Ford employees. They discovered, for example, that the company had one policy for delivering merit planning for 50,000 salaried workers in southern Michigan and 13 or 14 different systems on which to deliver that information. To build the portal, all those applications would have to be made Internet-ready.

The team pushed forward and HR Online was officially launched in January 1999. In a short time, HR Online was serving 75,000 employees in the United States, the United Kingdom, and Germany, and plans continued to grow the portal around the entire globe. "The functionality for the portal was very good from the start," Cooper says. "And the hit buildup was incredible. It's now the most accessed piece of the Ford Internet."

Cooper expects to have 100 percent of eligible employees using the portal by 2002. "It has changed the way we do business," he says. It was the existence of the HR Online portal that convinced Ford leaders like now retired CEO Jacques Nasser of the value of the Model E program, an ambitious effort to give away personal computers, printers, and Internet access to all Ford employees. To make the portal truly effective, access became a critical issue.

Currently, Ford managers are doing compensation planning, stock option planning, bonus planning, recruiting, and long-term incentive planning for all management personnel around the world through the portal. Managers are able to provide performance ratings to employees and view all employee personnel information via the portal. Salaried employees can update personal information and find answers to specific HR questions such as the status of health benefits and retirement plans. One key advantage: Employees are responsible and accountable for much of their personal data. By the end of 2001, managers were able to transfer, promote, and terminate employees themselves, directly through the portal.

Cooper acknowledges that the move to HR Online required letting go of decades of entrenched business practices. "Change is very painful," he concedes. "But we're now able to do things much faster and more efficiently. It is a change that is clearly transformational."

Bipin Patel, Ford's director of management systems, says employee satisfaction is on the rise. People find that when they can update their own information and access data themselves, the integrity of that data goes up exponentially. "You get efficiencies because you are not passing it three or four times. What people get is genuine," Patel says.

Of course, in a company as large as Ford, nothing happens quickly. Hourly employees have yet to be affected by the HR portal. Comparable capabilities to serve that part of the population will be rolled out over the next few years. "Eventually, we'll have one portal for every employee to get everything from any function, whether it's business, accounting, HR, manufacturing, or marketing," Cooper says. "It's not a five-year dream. It will happen sooner than that."

Cooper offers several key lessons he has learned from the portal effort:

- → *Manage expectations.* It is not an easy road to a successful implementation, so managing expectations of the key stakeholders—customers and team members—is essential.

- → *Get alignment.* The answer is not as important as having the right alignment in place to get you to the answer.

- → *It's not about the technology.* It's about understanding business practices, requirements, and how to deliver. At Ford, it's how you standardize, centralize, and reengineer business processes to use the technology. The technology itself is "the last two or three innings of the ballgame."

- → *Find a champion outside the area where the change is occurring.* Either the CEO or a very senior corporate executive must champion the cause. The champion can't come from IT or from HR itself. The champion must be from the customer base driving the change.

As HR Online was becoming a reality in 1999, Jacques Nasser took over the top job at Ford. He quickly saw B2E as a far broader concept than simply business to employee. The portal would soon emerge as a bridge to *business to the enterprise* and, eventually, morph into a platform for *business to everything*.

EXPELLING THE DINOSAURS

In April 2000, Nasser was invited to speak at an e-commerce gathering in New York City. The conference, sponsored by *Fortune* magazine and Goldman Sachs, was called "Battle Royale," and it was designed to be a forum for discussion between old-economy and new-economy companies about their views of the Internet and the future of business.

Nasser was pleased to be invited, believing that with all the e-business initiatives under way within Ford, he was being called in as a new-economy visionary. "But it turns out, they were inviting me there as one of the dinosaurs," Nasser recalled with a grimace. Nasser went on to make a strong presentation about Ford's embrace of the Internet, but the moment smarted for a long time.

"I knew we weren't a dinosaur company," Nasser said. "To be viewed as an old-fashioned company that doesn't get the technology . . . I knew that wasn't us. You go back to Henry Ford, our founder. We're inventors, we're creators. We love technology. We embrace technology as long as it is relevant to the consumer and delivers bottom-line results for our shareholders." Not that he needed it, but the conference served as a burr to get Nasser going. If his passion for turning Ford into a significant B2E company hadn't already been turned up high, it was now.

When Nasser became Ford's CEO in January 1999, e-business became one of the company's top priorities. Nasser's predecessor, Alex Trotman, had already paved the way by restructuring Ford into a global company and embracing technology as the binding threads for his ambitious effort. Like Trotman, Nasser got the Internet quickly and saw its potential for transforming Ford from its century-old roots as a transaction-based manufacturing bureaucracy into a streamlined, Internet-savvy giant focused on the customer. Even while the dot-com fury was at its height, Nasser believed that companies like Ford, rather than the ill-prepared start-ups, would gain the most from incorporating the Internet into the corporate fabric.

Nasser loudly disagreed with the notion of a new economy versus an old economy. "This is not about competing economic models but how to effectively use new technology to create new business possibilities," Nasser told the conference attendees. "Old economy? New economy? Who cares? The whole question of old versus new is so dated—and so last century. I prefer to look at what is happening as a convergence, a transformation, and a realignment of relationships—all delightful opportunities."

He also strongly believed that companies such as Ford, with its global presence, array of strong brands, excess of intellectual capital, and capability to absorb and utilize new technologies in a myriad of ways, will emerge among the winners in the B2E era.

What intrigued Nasser was the technology's potential to integrate the functions of the company in ways that could only be dreamed about in the past. He'd observed the years of struggle that came before digitized processes could be introduced within specific functions like finance or manufacturing. But suddenly, here was the Internet, a technology that is nimble, quick, relatively cheap, "that enables you to integrate the company across all business processes. That, to me, is the essence of B2E."

RELEASING THE E-POWER

Like HP, Ford is serious about its digital makeover. Before Nasser assumed the top post, Ford had begun a massive transformation into a global company, no easy task for a 100-year-old industrial giant. Nasser inherited a company in the nascent stages of its own reinvention, and he quickly grasped the power of technology in facilitating this makeover.

In 1999, Nasser decided to take an active role in putting the Internet to work for the company, as opposed to letting the new technology around the Internet and e-commerce infiltrate itself randomly. As General Motors was creating its e-GM unit, Ford unveiled its Ford ConsumerConnect division as a way to centralize its e-business activities. He also believed that if he left the company's e-initiatives to the traditional IT organization, its vast potential to touch every part of the organization would never be realized.

Though so many executives toss the online activities to the CIO, Nasser fervently believed that e-business was part of the fabric of the operating units. Therefore, the CIO would provide input, but the business units themselves have to make e-business an integrated part of their lives. Ford executives ensured the company's success in this endeavor by steeping themselves in the technology, speaking directly to technology industry leaders in the Silicon Valley. Ford executives like Trotman, Nasser, and now William Clay Ford, Jr., are able to see the broad potential of the Internet to fundamentally change the way Ford does business. They realize there is a fine balance between rigid technology standardization and complete anarchy. They have placed a premium on innovation and experimentation. Because no one knew what would work and what wouldn't, there was a tremendous amount of encouragement to try different things.

Nasser, for example, was hesitant to set anything in stone at the outset. "No one knew who the winners would be," he said about the cornucopia of technologies surrounding the Internet. "There was good value in trying different things without standardizing on a system that may or may not be the best," he explained.

One of the other risks of standardization was the potential of standardizing on the lowest common denominator. With so many varying levels of skills and competencies throughout the organization, that risk had to be considered. On the other hand, Ford realized, you can't have a complete lack of discipline. A company can't risk losing the economies of scale it has. It has got to have a strategy and be aligned around that strategy.

In that regard, the company began to embrace global governance of its new hub portal and other e-business initiatives. Setting the strategy and the basic direction helped determine the allocation of resources and made the company's priorities clear.

Less than two years into the effort, Ford leaders echo what other successful executives believe: E-business *is* business. Ford places e-business in the same category as quality, customer satisfaction, productivity, supplier relations, and people development. In other words, it is simply table stakes to the game.

As Ford became deeply immersed in its e-business efforts, several important lessons emerged:

→ E-business must be made a top corporate priority by the CEO.

→ Speed is of the essence.

→ Nothing happens without a carefully detailed vision.

→ E-business must be viewed as part of the business, not as a separate project.

→ Strong partners should be brought in early, but too many partners can spoil the e-broth.

→ Creativity and nimbleness must be tempered by hard, practical business parameters.

→ CEOs must embrace a new way to lead.

When he first became CEO, for example, Nasser began a weekly e-mail letter to the company's 350,000 employees. Though it might seem mundane, these "Let's Chat" e-mails, regular Friday afternoon electronic missives that went out to employees in all 160 countries in which Ford competes, became a potent tool in shifting the Ford culture from a set of regional organizations to a single, global entity. It also bears the message to Ford employees about how high a priority e-business has become.

It is not difficult to imagine the influence of "Let's Chat" in a giant global enterprise where the CEO has traditionally been a distant, unseen figure, more myth than reality. "I was working in Asia-Pacific operations and the impact was incredible," says Bipin Patel. "People in Taiwan felt as connected as people in Australia and people in the U.S. to the Ford Motor Company. He would tell us how he met with analysts today and here is what we talked about, or how he test drove a new model that's coming out in Europe, or reviewed operations in China. For a person six or seven layers down in the organization to get this information directly from the CEO is a big thing, especially for a company steeped in 100 years of tradition."

Perhaps more crucial, the e-mails told Ford employees in a heretofore impossible way that the CEO "is accessible and interested," according to W. James Fish, retired executive director. "He shared his thoughts and activities with us and we felt we could go back to him, person to person, with our views, including dissenting views."

The e-mails also "showed everyone that the CEO and the leadership of the company were serious about e-business," added Patel. "It wasn't just something that was here today, gone tomorrow. It made it a lot easier for us to drive a whole host of B2E processes. The message from the top was that this was key for our company's transformation."

REINVENTION IN DIFFICULT TIMES

Like HP's Fiorina, Nasser tried to transform Ford under significant duress. After a brief honeymoon with Wall Street in 1999, in which Ford turned in better-than-expected financial results and Nasser was named Automotive Industries Man of the Year, Ford's fortunes have recently slipped. In late 2001, Nasser was asked to resign. William Clay Ford, Jr., took over as CEO.

It marked the latest in a series of difficult tests for the company. After a series of fatal accidents involving Ford Explorers and Firestone Wilderness tires, Ford and Firestone faced a $3 billion recall of all Firestone tires on Ford vehicles. After some public finger-pointing on both sides, the 85-year relationship came to an abrupt end as Ford and Firestone parted ways.

In the midst of this public relations quagmire, Nasser faced even stiffer challenges in the marketplace. As the global economy started to sour, Ford saw declining profits, higher marketing costs, slipping market share, and a raft of cost-cutting measures, including production cuts and massive layoffs. The crucial North American market grew even more competitive and by late 2001, Ford's shares were trading near their 52-week low. Nasser made several key management shifts to try to shake up the company's efforts. It was clearly not enough.

As if all this had not been daunting enough, Ford, like the rest of American industry, then faced the aftermath of the tragic terrorist attacks in New York and Washington, D.C. As we write this, it is impossible to predict how global markets will react and when and if stability will return us to business as usual anytime soon.

Nothing, however, could derail Ford's commitment to its e-business initiative; in fact, Ford remains committed to becoming a top B2E player. If anything, the power of e-business became more apparent to Ford executives and they named e-business, along with customer satisfaction, the two *breakthrough strategic priorities* at Ford.

Indeed, in the midst of the Firestone crisis, Nasser took his top management team for a two-day visit to the Silicon Valley to learn firsthand from Cisco Systems about their successful embrace of the Internet. The group met with John Chambers, Cisco's CEO, along with his top executives to discuss doing business online.

According to *Business2.0* magazine, the meeting helped Ford managers begin to understand how a company's entire operation could be built around the Internet. Martin Inglis, Ford's CFO and formerly head of North American operations, said he had a "wow moment" when Carl Redfield, Cisco's head of manufacturing, explained how he used the Internet to run the company's assembly operations on a build-to-order basis. "It was so fundamentally different than our business," Inglis told *Business2.0*. "I got it."[1]

All of Ford's top managers got it, as a matter of fact. They believe that e-business brings speed, reduces complexity, increases sales, and eliminates inefficiencies. The Internet serves to unlock the full intellectual capital of Ford Motor Company. With $180 billion in revenues, Ford is the fourth largest company on the Fortune 500 list and fifth in the size of its employee population. Transforming such a behemoth is no simple task, and Ford understands this long journey requires a long-term commitment.

Rather than stirring the expected resistance to such a transformation, Ford's B2E efforts have been met mostly with enthusiasm. Because Ford leaders insisted on providing strategic frameworks for the efforts and instituted clear ideas about governance and regular e-reviews, the path has been far smoother than might be expected at such a large organization. If anything, people are asking for more and asking how quickly they can move.

FORD CONSUMERCONNECT

Already, Ford has embraced e-technologies for key internal and external needs. In 2000, Ford launched ConsumerConnect, a unit designed to coordinate all of the company's e-business activities. Brian Kelley, a young, aggressive former GE executive, was brought in to run the unit and spearhead the company's e-commerce efforts. Beyond his charisma and youthful energy, Kelley's hiring sent a strong message inside Ford that the company was serious about e-business, serious enough to look outside of Ford for the best possible candidate. He is now president of Lincoln/Mercury.

Not only did Ford launch one of the auto industry's first HR portals, called HR Online, in 1999, but Ford has also put its credit application process online, introduced wireless technology in its plants, put payroll and employee information online, and digitized purchasing operations. Ford estimates that these efforts saved the company hundreds of millions of dollars in 2000 and more the following year.

Ford also weathered the short but ferocious onslaught of the dot-com era when aggressive newcomers like Carsdirect.com and Autobytel.com shone in the Internet spotlight. During that period, dealers viewed the Internet as the enemy and believed these start-ups were attempting to usurp their traditional business. In hindsight, these dot-com companies had no chance of ever replacing the retail distribution system, because they just didn't have the community contact, the relationships, and the sales and service experience that customers demanded.

But the dot-com hysteria provided a much-needed wake-up call. What began as a series of defensive maneuvers has emerged as a competitive edge for Ford. For example, Ford pumped up its Ford.com web site for customers, allowing customers to shop online, find the exact model, make, color and style, along with the nearest dealer who can provide the vehicle. In 2000, more than 124 million unique visitors clicked on the web site, generating nearly $1 billion in revenue. Late in 2000, the company launched FordDirect.com, a separate company formed in partnership with Ford Division dealers to bring direct, online sales to customers. In the first few months, more than 80 percent of dealers in the United States joined the new partnership.

In the midst of that experience, yet another positive outcome emerged. Like other carmakers, Ford had never really known or tracked its customers. With up to 80 percent of its data sitting on mainframes in Ford data centers, there was no efficient, real-time access to all that invaluable customer information. Somewhere between the dealer and the corporation, the customer's profile—what they bought, when they bought it, what they liked, how often they'd returned for further purchases—evaporated.

According to *Business2.0,* "For years, Ford has shipped cars to dealerships, while salespeople sold the cars and kept greasy index cards about who bought what. While Ford Credit financed the cars, and Ford's customer service division tracked warranty information, Ford had no institutional memory, no central way to capture details of the relationship with a customer."[2] A lifelong Taurus owner who decided to buy a Mustang for his college-aged daughter, for example, would be considered a first-time customer as far as Ford Motor Company was concerned, a remarkable fumble of relationship marketing opportunities.

Now, with Percepta, a joint venture with a company called Teletech, Ford is transforming its global call centers into customer relationship centers. The goal is to use Percepta's web-based capability to build a customer knowledge system to manage all customer interfaces in an integrated, efficient, and value-added manner. Basically, the system culls consumer data on 40 million Ford customers from Ford's 250 web sites, its dealer network, and other sources, and it organizes the information in a central database. "When car owners call about a loan or a recall or a new model, Ford now has a means to capture that information and log it into a 'datamart' accessible from all points in the company: marketing executives, designers, finance managers, and (Ford executives)," says *Business2.0*.[3]

At the same time, Ford joined General Motors and Daimler/Chrysler in the much-publicized Covisint online supplier exchange. In the first five months of operation, Covisint held more than 150 auction events, generating a transaction volume of nearly $1 billion.

All this, impressive as it is for a so-called dinosaur, was merely the prologue for Ford's transformation. And if Fiorina faced a thousand tribes when she arrived at HP, Nasser encountered ten thousand at Ford. If Ford was not as culturally autonomous as HP, its sheer size and structure made it, in many key ways, more amorphous than most other companies.

Ford has long been a collection of autonomous brands—Lincoln, Mercury, Volvo, Jaguar, Mazda, Land Rover, Hertz, along with business units like Ford Credit.

Ford's 100-year-old business model was based on functional silos mixed with a raft of constituencies, such as multitiers of suppliers, dealers, and consumers. Under Nasser's predecessor, Alex Trotman, Ford had committed itself to globalize the company, a necessary but wrenching cultural change that made Nasser's path even more difficult to travel.

MODEL E

Nonetheless, unlike many CEOs who pay lip service to the power of technology, Nasser put his money where his mouth was and set in motion a program unprecedented in a company of Ford's size and reach. The key to globalization and the successful integration of e-business inside a company as large as Ford is *access,* Nasser realized.

He knew that many of the company's employees simply had no way to connect to the Internet or even to the company itself. In a company where the influence of technology is ever increasing, it is crucial that employees understand the technology. So in 2000, he kicked off "Model E," a three-year global initiative in which every Ford employee is to be given a free desktop PC and printer for his or her home, along with Internet access for $5 a month.

To truly transform Ford, Nasser believed that all of his employees must be fully aware of and involved with the Internet age. The company already had more than 100,000 workstations for its employees at their offices, but "why should that stop at the office?" Nasser asked. "Why don't we connect with each other whether you're here or at home? And by the way, how can we also make that connection with the family, so that employees are not only communicating with the company but with each other?"

Steve Paschen, director of the Model E program, says the goal of the program is three C's: (1) competency, (2) communications, and (3) consumers. By offering technology for free, employees with little or no access to PCs or the Internet will now be able to gain a level of competency on the Internet. With this equipment in their homes, Ford will be better able to communicate with employees and they with each other. And in exposing employees to the Internet, they will better understand how consumers are using the web to change their lives.

The idea of work/life flexibility is a huge factor in Ford's vision. The Model E program, which was put on hold due to the economic difficulties when Nasser resigned, had a strong emphasis on the families. Very often it is the children who are opening parents' eyes to the power of the Internet, and by allowing the entire family to become better versed in what is happening online, it will make for more informed employees. Ford believes that with 350,000 employees, if every employee is a little bit more aware of the marketplace, a little bit more literate in this new technology, and can communicate better, the leverage is huge.

"It isn't about reducing costs," Nasser said about the program. "In fact, that is almost incidental in the longer term. The truth is, we feel fundamentally that this is good for us. It's about doing business better and more quickly, integrating the business and ending up with people who are more aware and can make better business decisions. Trying to measure this would be like trying to calculate the benefits of having telephones."

Paschen says nearly 200,000 U.S.-based employees have already participated in the plan. "There's no cost benefit analysis on this," he says. "We believed in our hearts that there would be value to employees, families, communities and to the company. At the end of the day, that justifies the cost of the program."

INTERNET INSIDE

The beginnings of Ford's e-vision predate Nasser's rise to CEO by several years. In the mid-1990s, his predecessor, Alex Trotman, decided that Ford, which was then a collection of 20 separate companies all sporting the Ford logo, would become a single, global corporation. To survive and grow into the future, Ford had to leverage its size and scale in effective new ways. The company began an aggressive push to standardize work practices around the globe. One of the crucial ways to enable this massive change was to start moving work to the world wide web.

At the same time that HR Online was being formulated, Ford launched an internal intranet that would eventually provide services for the personal needs of employees. Under the umbrella strategy called "Internet Inside," this new hub portal, called MyFord.com, will offer a way to balance company, personal, and job needs. Already, more than 170,000 Ford employees in 800 facilities and 150 manufacturing plants worldwide have made MyFord.com a part of their everyday work life. When all of its varied pieces are in place, this hub portal will act as a central gateway to all personalized information, all internally and externally stored information, and as a connection to Ford's business strategy.

Bipin Patel, who is overseeing the development of the hub portal, says the project is about halfway to completion, though in fact, the portal is such a living entity that its growth and development are truly an open-ended endeavor. It is no simple task, because it will encompass more than 1,000 internal and external web sites and 1 million documents.

Ford is already calling its portal the largest corporate personalization portal yet launched. With HR Online and other subportals, the hub portal will become a repository of all HR, flex benefits, performance grading, development, and learning needs. Self-service is the underlying foundation and raison d'être. Job needs will also be served by disintermediating critical functions. If a revenue analyst in a particular business unit needs financial data, he or she will get that data directly without having to talk to the finance people.

Patel says that the personalization portal is already in place and functioning. Integrating job needs is the next phase, and his group is at work incorporating more of the legacy applications onto the portal so that Ford can reap the benefits of its human capital in new and unexpected ways.

Ford sees tremendous benefit from the work/life balance that the portal is intended to achieve. For example, the company recently opened a satellite work center north of its Dearborn headquarters, closer to where many employees live. The work center has become extremely popular in a short time because it provides the same facilities and access as headquarters but closer to home so that employees can spend more quality time with their families.

The center is also an excellent testing ground for collaborative tools like e-room and net-meeting. Patel says that the long-range goal is to fully understand the day in the life of each employee. What is the day in the life of an engineer like? What does she do? How do we recruit her? What is her role? How does she grow as a manager? How does she develop herself? And what are her needs and the company's needs—day to day, hour to hour, minute to minute—to get the job done?

"That's the next phase of making this a genuine B2Everything initiative within the company," Patel says. "We can now start pushing the envelope."

Patel acknowledges that rolling the portal out around the world "is a constant struggle." Speed of execution, scalability, and rolling it out across brands vary from one country to the next. Patel speaks of continuous learning and says he has concluded that the B2E effort is really "never complete."

According to Patel, the Cisco visit gave people a strategic framework with which to evaluate and, in some cases, validate what Ford is doing. Borrowing liberally from Cisco's *Net Readiness* concepts (a book authored by two Cisco Internet executives, which was read widely throughout Ford), the leaders of Ford's B2E transformation asked themselves, "Are we doing webification? Are we achieving operational excellence and rational experimentation? Do we have any breakthrough projects?"[4]

Ford's IT organization must deliver value every three to four months to the business. Projects can no longer have one- or two-year time frames; the Internet economy simply moves too fast for that.

The second part of ruthless execution is called *systems development life cycle* (SDLC), which employs a six-stage cycle—from analysis to launch—that includes business partner involvement and constant gate reviews along the way. The third step is *operations reviews with senior management on a regular basis.*

From all of this, Patel says, a set of lessons has emerged:

→ Changing the corporate culture is difficult but possible only if the CEO sets the direction and champions the effort.

→ Bottom-line savings and profits must be identified early.

→ In a company as large and diverse as Ford, a phased launch strategy is key.

→ A governance process is essential.

→ Constant delivery and ruthless execution are the keys to making the vision a reality.

"It's not a question of today, we're an old economy company, tomorrow we're new," Patel says. "It's really about how you embrace the pieces of the new economy and become that company that's constantly innovative and experimenting and learning and growing as it goes."

SHAPING THE FUTURE

Ford has embraced the B2E concept because its vision of the future goes well beyond portals and e-business initiatives. What is already clear is that this isn't about the Internet, handheld devices, PCs, or cellular phones. What it is about is a future in which all of these things become so imbedded in the way we work and live, in our homes and businesses, that it will simply be part of the fabric of everything we do.

"If you look at a typical car or truck ten years into the future, there's going to be an incredible change in the communication, safety, navigation, and entertainment capabilities imbedded in that vehicle," Patel predicts. "There will be almost total transparency between the workplace, your transportation and your home. Today, we have telephones in our homes, offices, cars. We've got fax machines and workstations and laptops and Palm Pilots and each has a different phone number. They are each interesting technologies but not very well linked together. In the future, they will be."

And at the same time, such integration will also move invisibly but quickly across the functions and business processes of the company "to the point where the lines will be totally fused together. We won't think of manufacturing, logistics or engineering, they will all be integrated seamlessly," he says.

As Ford attempts to regain its former glory, it is a very different company than the one founded by Henry Ford at the beginning of the twentieth century. Yet there are connections from the past century to the one we've just begun. The Model T changed the world because it was easy to use and affordable. The Internet is changing the world through ease of use and affordability as well. Instead of assembly lines of auto parts, the Internet offers information to anyone, anywhere, anytime they want it. In this way, it has replaced mass production with mass customization and, in so doing, will remake the concept of work much as the Model T remade the idea of transportation.

CHAPTER FIVE

PricewaterhouseCoopers

Ironically, perhaps the most challenging portal implementation that we've encountered is within our own firm, PricewaterhouseCoopers (PwC). Though we are the largest professional services firm in the world, PwC is embracing the B2E concept with the creation of an ambitious global portal that will do nothing less than transform the way we work and the way the firm does business.

Of course, like most companies where knowledge and ideas are the product, PwC already had an award-winning internal information portal, called *Knowledge-Curve*. Partners and staff of PwC employ a mobile way of working that provides its global staff—equipped with laptops—secure access to the intranet, virtually anywhere in the world.

But as good as KnowledgeCurve has been, it does not provide the global infrastructure that is necessary to meet the firm's client and staff requirements for the next 10 years. As we looked to the Internet to go beyond pure information sharing—into transaction processing, e-learning, and collaboration beyond the firm's boundaries—the technology and governance of Knowledge-Curve was simply insufficient. If we are to maintain a competitive edge going forward, we needed to build a place where 90 percent or more of the staff from around the world would visit every day. This global "water-cooler" will be where the power of portals and a secure infrastructure will be unleashed and change the way we work.

"Moving any organization, including Pricewater-houseCoopers, toward the digital frontier is a formidable task," says Samuel A. DiPiazza, PwC's newly named global CEO. "It demands both a sense of urgency and the courage to champion deep cultural change. But B2E is not as much a technology as it is a transformation. It has the power to reshape how people work and how they relate to each other, their companies, and their customers. We believe our portal will create an intimacy and loyalty with our client base that goes far beyond anything we've seen before."

As this was written in late 2001, firms like PwC were in the middle of an economic slowdown that put real pressure on IT and other infrastructure costs. Nevertheless, PwC invested more than $25 million to modernize its portal and security infrastructure because we realized that this effort is not discretionary, it is core to the business.

Like other companies making this journey, PwC's portal initiative is a multiyear effort that is already paying dividends. Despite the firm's unorthodox organizational framework, we've decided to include PwC as a case study in this book because we believe there are valuable lessons to be learned from the complexities of building a portal within a professional services firm. Let us assure you, we are not the cobbler's children.

However, because of the structure of our massive global firm and the way it operates, we are, in some ways, forced to tell clients the old saw, "Do as we say, not as we do." For example, PwC is unlike HP, Ford, and most other corporate hierarchies. As with many professional services firms, PwC is a giant partnership, owned by its partners and run with a matrix style of management. The current firm was born on July 1, 1998, with the merger of two Big Six accounting firms, Price Waterhouse and Coopers & Lybrand. No merger of this size is simple or without significant organizational issues, and we've struggled at times incorporating two diverse cultures into one.

Our 150,000 employees in 150 countries work in a partnership structure characterized by lines of service, industries, and territories. In fact, while all PwC partners share in the income of the entire firm, it is actually a group of partnerships, each owned by partners in the country in which the offices are located. While Sam DiPiazza is our CEO, it is not a traditional command-and-control position, so achieving firmwide consensus on almost anything, especially a complex, cataclysmic technology like a portal, is a challenge at best. In addition, our tax and audit business is quite distinct from our management consulting services business, PwC Consulting. It is no secret that the firm has actively sought ways to split the two groups into separate companies in recent years. A plan to merge the consulting business with HP in 2000 made headlines around the world, but the deal was never consummated.

In fact, if there is consensus on anything, it is the belief among those building the PwC portal that the firm is both its best and worst client rolled into one. Indeed, if we can build a successful portal for ourselves, we can do it for anyone. There is strong incentive to move in this direction. If we can create an online destination where 90

percent or more of the staff visits every day, the portal
will have a huge impact on:

→ *Corporate communication.* We'd get rid of
the redundancy and mixed messages that
travel throughout the firm.

→ *Collaboration.* Imagine how communication changes when you know someone will
see the same thing as you in real time or near
real time.

→ *E-enabling.* Enabling the company.

→ *Cost savings.* PricewaterhouseCoopers will
save millions of dollars each year in real
estate and travel costs because its global con-
nectivity allows people to work anywhere on
any device.

→ *More cost savings.* The firm seeks to save
more millions each year on operating
expenses by moving transactions to the web.

All of this can happen only if the portal attracts
nearly all the members of our community and offers easy
access and a secure infrastructure. Unlike carmakers or
computer suppliers, the product of professional services
firms is knowledge, and knowledge is an entity that is
tailor-made for sharing and selling via the Internet. Using
web-based B2E capabilities, PwC can leverage its vast and
deep well of information and ideas for its customers,
employees, and business partners in ways that were
heretofore impossible.

If one thinks of a firm like PwC as a vast repository of
thought leadership, multifaceted expertise, tools, and peer-
to-peer communities, the Holy Grail has long been the creation of a common global platform that brings all these

resources together under a single, collaborative umbrella for clients and employees. "Think of the portal as sitting on top of all that information and serving as a single doorway into the PwC experience," says Kersten Lanes, the PwC partner in charge of the portal's implementation.

While the Internet has exponentially increased the banks of knowledge within our corporate universe, it has also increased the complexity that comes with sharing that knowledge. With its size and scope, PwC, not unlike other professional services firms, has a relatively high turnover. The firm is constantly renewing and refreshing our employee base and the old Rolodex model no longer works for effective knowledge sharing. Properly used, the portal will be the great new enabler of knowledge sharing and, in turn, is an incredibly powerful communications vehicle.

Lanes calls the portal the "global glue" that eventually will serve to keep a giant, fragmented firm like PwC together. The Internet is an incredible unifier, she says, a single point that is global, transparent, available 24-7, and brings together the firm in a way that is otherwise impossible. In a company that has long prided itself on local control and autonomy, the portal is both a global tether and a conduit to collaboration and the deep mining and sharing of information.

In so doing, the portal allows PwC to be recognized in the marketplace as being a mile deep as well as miles wide. Both employees and clients will be able to gain easy access to our knowledge, our insight, and our array of published material to suit their unique interests. It will allow us to revamp our training processes—shifting from the costly and time-consuming physical movement of people to offering global training online via the portal.

In addition, the portal becomes a way for younger and newer employees to tap into the experiential wisdom of the firm in a way that is filtered and organized. Though we've got many 20- and 30-year employees, we also know that the reality of today's workforce is that many of our professionals will spend only part of their careers here. Yet we need them to have access to the knowledge that will allow them to serve our clients like seasoned veterans. The most important thing the portal does, in effect, is empower our people to bring better and more comprehensive solutions to their clients.

And the payoffs are real and tangible. After decades of spending hundreds of millions on IT with often inconsistent results, the portal allows the firm to replace its internal communications infrastructure with the public infrastructure, the Internet. "This is a gigantic business opportunity," says Robert Bleimeister, the e-business strategy partner. "The cost savings associated with doing this over the Internet are enormous." In reality, we will still spend millions of dollars more than before to support the portal, but the key difference is that we will get much greater bang for this buck.

Bleimeister also expects significant leaps in productivity as our people get to the right information when they need it, wherever they are located. This is a huge benefit because we at PwC are essentially new-millennium nomads, moving between home and client sites; working on planes, trains, and automobiles; rarely spending time in our offices sitting at desks. Access to timely data and to each other are the keys to our success.

Not only will the portal be geographically neutral, it will interface seamlessly with any type of device, from a desktop PC to a wireless PDA or cell phone and whatever new form of computing comes down the pike. In a firm like PwC, where only 14 percent of the U.S. staff has assigned desks and everyone gets cell phones and laptops instead of desktops, the ability to arm this mobile workforce in this manner is a huge competitive advantage. In fact, as it acts as a doorway *and* a pathway, the portal will also profile the visitor, whether an employee or client, so that the organization can figure out what is important to that individual and get it for them in a seamless fashion, whether they are in Boston or Berlin.

Long a technology pioneer, PwC has already compiled an impressive array of web-based services, such as DELTA, the Tax and Legal Services group's online document, knowledge, and workflow system; and myWashingtonTaxOffice, the online community of Washington National Tax Services. As we said earlier, our internal knowledge network, KnowledgeCurve, has grown into an effective intranet in its own right. All of these services will be recast as content on the finished portal.

James C. Emerson, editor of the *Professional Services Review*, writes,

> When you consider that PwC is at the beginning of its digital roadmap and its internet solutions project is only in its early development stage, it is remarkable how many natural applications have already been uncovered and implemented.
>
> It is hard to imagine a professional services firm that didn't have some data collection, knowledge management, collaboration or analysis and reporting function that will not benefit from using the internet. We would have to argue with Jack Welch who said the internet was tailor made for GE; the internet appears to be tailor made for the largest professional services firms.[1]

THE LAND OF A THOUSAND SILOS
Like most other organizations, PwC did not discover the Internet overnight. Instead, awareness of the potential of this powerful new medium spread across the firm in the

late 1990s, with a myriad of credible ideas germinating in different practices and various lines of business. Both before and after the merger, ambitious partners began to embrace the web, build intranets and client extranets to serve their needs, and quickly there appeared a new and increasingly disjointed landscape around the world. Like at HP, the autonomous nature of the company created a multitude of confusing and often conflicting initiatives in the B2Customer (B2C), B2B, and B2E environments.

"We became the land of a thousand silos," says Michael Willis, PwC partner in the Assurance and Business Advisory Services IT group. "The problem is that you are forced to search through these silos to find what you need to do your job. Actually getting the user to the right silo when they need to be there became a nightmare. And on top of that are the back-end maintenance and management issues that accompany this kind of environment."

PricewaterhouseCoopers has taken a different approach by deliberately converging its web infrastructure across the B2B, B2C, and B2E domains. While many companies run these initiatives as separate programs, and indeed they typically have different customers and business value, PwC recognizes the value and synergy of looking at a common web infrastructure that can serve all three domains. We do this by focusing on the similarities (e.g., usage tracking/reporting, personalization, application integration, content searching, customization (profiling), collaboration, authentication, authorization, and content delivery) while also recognizing such differences as security, commerce processing, compliance, and access.

It didn't take long for corporate visionaries like Keith Wishon, the CIO of the firm's audit business; Gerald Leener, CIO of the firm's tax business; Howard Niden, CIO of PwC Consulting; Ken Cooke, e-business leader in the United States; Ed Smith, e-business leader in the United Kingdom; and others to see the potential of a single, firmwide portal to create an umbrella over this maze of web sites and intranets. Not surprising, many of our first e-business leaders have business, not IT, back-grounds. We purposely didn't hire technologists and place them in the IT hierarchy, reporting to a CIO. We sought respected partners like Lanes, Smith, and Cooke, who knew how to operate by consensus. They also understand that the charter is not about technology, but about transformation.

Portal planners were hardly starting with a clean slate. In our matrix of external and internal lines of ser-vice [e.g., Assurance and Business Advisory Services (ABAS), PwC Consulting, and Tax and Legal Services (TLS)], there were as many as 85 portal projects under way around the globe. The TLS had built the Tax News Network and later created Mindlink, a global B2C site that offered tax-related information to PwC clients. The ABAS had both myclient.com and mypwc.com among its Internet plans. PwC Consulting had its own enterprise-wide web effort, and of course, there was KnowledgeCurve.

As the focus on corporate portals began to prolifer-ate and our concept of B2E came to the firm's attention, future shock began to set in. If we didn't gain consensus on a single global portal, we'd be leading the firm down a hundred dead-end streets. The challenge was even tougher because each line of business had its own unique goals for the portal. Beyond that, we had to maintain ongoing sites for the users even as we built a single portal.

As the forces inside the firm began to recognize where we were and where we needed to go, it became clear that our effort was akin to trying to change the tires on a race-car without pulling into the pit stop. What was needed was some solid up-front planning and a vision. Starting in

2000, the firm, in a rare instance of international consensus, came together to form a global e-business council with 20 members. A portal steering committee with eight members was spun off from the council.

Kersten Lanes insisted on writing down a specific mission statement. "Even though people might have believed that they all knew what it was going to say, I suggested 'If you don't know what the scope of the project is, you won't know if you are successful,' " Lanes says. "We want to know when we've climbed the mountain and we can't know that until we all agree that this is what we are trying to accomplish." The portal steering committee agreed, and the mission statement emerged:

> The mission of the PwC Portal is to enhance our connectivity and relationships with clients and staff. We will generate revenue through innovative service delivery and support staff performance through enhanced knowledge and information sharing. We will achieve cost savings and improve user experience through shared infrastructure and common standards. This will strengthen our corporate image as a global integrated professional services firm while allowing underlying businesses flexibility to meet specific market needs.

Unlike traditional corporate hierarchies such as HP, where Carly Fiorina can mandate such a mission, the distributed structure of PwC makes such a mission statement quite remarkable, if not revolutionary. By late 2000, the firm's senior partners agreed that a single portal must be created and that all other individual efforts had to be shut down or incorporated into the main portal. At the same time, the portal planners understood that you cannot simply mandate away the very autonomy that is the signature of the firm.

For example, the steering committee recognized early on that the project leaders within each line of business had to own the project themselves. If they didn't have responsibility, it would be an easy and natural route to use Lanes as a scapegoat should things get bogged down. What emerged, therefore, was a blend—a streamlined core infrastructure with a narrow band of top-notch global functionality. Everything else remained decentralized. Sam DiPiazza, CEO of PwC, realized early on that moving any organization toward the digital frontier would require a bias for action and a sense of urgency in the entire business. He also knew that deep cultural change was an inevitable result.

Those who lead the portal effort will admit that, despite the mandate from the firm's executive partners to merge all efforts, the corporate infighting and turf battles have often been brutal. Lanes says, "In PwC, respect for the individual is so strong that it is often hard to get consensus." The competitive nature of the partners was so intense, she says, that it often resulted in a "Noah's Ark" of committees—everything had to be done two-by-two so that competing voices would be heard. As a result, little was accomplished.

It wasn't until Wishon and Leener asked Lanes to oversee the project development that three key lines of service (ABAS, TLS, and PwC Consulting) gained traction in pooling their efforts. One critical success factor moving forward was to create a centralized budget under Lanes for the project. By taking the money away from each line of service, it forced them all to work together. With that, they gave Lanes the power to run the project, and with the authority to move the effort forward, little by little they were able to gain grudging consensus.

As James Emerson wrote in his *Professional Services Report,*

> The challenge is to convert more than 100 years
> of doing business another way into Web-based
> systems and processes that have been designed
> to a common global standard, on a common
> platform with a common look and feel. And this
> is not a challenge to treat lightly. The firm that
> successfully makes this transition will have a sig-
> nificant competitive advantage within a few
> years. The firms that ignore the challenge or end
> up with a hodgepodge of applications will look
> like dinosaurs in a few years.[2]

PwC is definitely not ignoring the challenge. The portal effort now has a life of its own due, if nothing else, to
the economies of scale that it offers to a firm our size. The
cost savings and productivity increases that emerge from
the use of the portal are at least four to five times the payback of any type of similar effort that isn't based upon
the Internet.

Beyond cost savings, the portal serves to flatten the
organization. "This is all about doing away with multiple
levels of infrastructure that are in place to collect and dis-
tribute information," Bleimeister says. He says that firms
such as PwC—global, 24-7, self-service types of businesses that rely on extraordinary expertise resident in its
individuals—will be the biggest beneficiaries of these portal efforts. "We've got lots and lots of smart people who
don't need multiple layers of management to operate,"
Bleimeister says.

Referring to a rival firm's recent television commercial that spoofed the work of consultants as one of herd-
ing cats, Bleimeister laughs and asks, "Why herd them? I

don't want to herd our cats. I want to unleash them. And to the extent that I find a resource—in our business it's usually another person—who can help me do my job, the portal can cut through all manner of garbage to get that resource aligned to help me represent a client."

UNLEASHING THE CATS

Consensus, shaky as it might be in a partnership, has allowed PwC to move forward aggressively with the portal effort. Key existing pieces are being transformed to fit the portal. For example, the firm is incorporating KnowledgeCurve, along with its customer-facing web site pwcglobal.com, and then adding a B2E element created from the work of the consulting side of the firm. The idea is to leverage as much as possible from existing systems and pull all this together under a single governance structure.

The B2E portion, which provides HR self-service functions, is perhaps the most challenging aspect of the project. The PwC organizations in each country have their own HR systems and financial systems. There is limited integration on a global basis, and thus it is difficult to leverage as much as the firm would like. This hasn't stopped Lanes and her crew from trying, however.

For Bleimeister, the key to implementing any kind of technology initiative "is the recognition that *you've got to get going.* I learned from software companies a long time ago that you get a version out there as quickly as you can. You don't spend an enormous amount of money making that happen. And then you listen to your customers and continue to iterate off what your customers tell you is important."

To overcome these challenges, PwC is developing a global template for B2E based on the B2E solution set developed for its client-facing efforts. This template and solution set provide a common architecture, standards, infrastructure, and organizational framework for the portal, while providing a federated (decentralized) approach to content management. Staff in Europe and the United States will find HR information in the same place, but the information they receive will be customized to their country, and the transactions will be routed to the country or regional back-end systems.

PricewaterhouseCoopers will save millions of dollars through this approach by eliminating the redundancy of having each country inventing its own solution, while still allowing countries considerable autonomy to implement the content they want and need.

We firmly believe, as a knowledge-based company, that portals will become more valuable, more useful, and more differentiated as we listen to our customers and build deep pockets of the very expertise they need. In fact, our very value is based on providing such knowledge management collaboration. A portal that becomes a virtual water cooler, where people gather to find their answers and seek such collaboration, is a key requirement.

In any difficult organizational shift, lessons emerge from the pain. For example, we have learned:

→ The technology always gets better, so you've got to believe in it and move quickly. Think of it as software development and the first iteration is version 1.0. Get something up and operating, listen to your customers, do the debugging, and make revisions along the way.

→ Make sure the people you ask to lead the portal effort are passionate and fully dedicated to the project and that its success is linked to the success of their careers. Avoid the hangers-on on such projects, the folks who invest 5 percent of their time but have opinions about everything. Trying to do this work part-time is almost always a recipe for disaster.

→ Get it done fast because big technology initiatives have limited staying power in a big company. In a large organization, staying the course on any firmwide initiative requires speed—30-, 60-, 90-day outputs—or it rarely reaches fruition. Unless the game plan is based on speed, a company tends to add time, effort, and bureaucracy to a project so that it never gets done.

Staying power is difficult to generate in tough economic times, which we are certainly experiencing as we write this book. The end of the dot-com boom followed by the collapse of the Nasdaq set off an extended economic slowdown, which eventually hit all sectors and industries. Along with everyone else, professional services firms have been hit hard with cost cutting and layoffs. Yet, we deeply believe that the time to make dramatic changes to an organization is when things are not going well. Trying to move giant initiatives through a complex organization when business is booming is extremely tough. "Why rock the boat," people ask.

On the other hand, when companies have to reexamine their cost structures, improve their productivity, and find a path to new prosperity, there is an opportunity to implement change. That only happens, of course, with a project that is on the corporate front burner and that has the backing of the executive management. PricewaterhouseCoopers's portal has that backing, which is essential to its growth and success.

Indeed, our consultants have seen that the difficult economy in the post-dot-com era has actually forced most big companies to put the brakes on technology spending on many fronts, such as enterprise resource platform (ERP) or customer resource management (CRM). However, because of the real promise of the portal to radically transform an organization and thus the bottom line, global portal initiatives remain very much in the hearts and minds of both CEOs and the IT community among our clients.

We believe that integrated information systems are, in fact, a cornerstone to lower Selling, General, and Administrative (SG&A) costs in the infrastructure of the future. A successful portal cannot be built upon spaghetti-like IT systems, and companies that have truly integrated their portal with sound underlying technology will reap huge benefits. *In fact, we believe the B2E portal is the key to unlock return on previous IT investments!*

We believe this because one lesson is inviolate: *People embrace what works.* When our portal is fully functional, available, and easy to access and navigate, our professionals will flock to it. There is already an insatiable desire among our professionals for more aggressive and robust online collaboration with our clients.

Though our clients value the historical, personal, one-on-one relationships we've established, we want to enrich and deepen those relationships with any other form of communication and collaboration we can embrace, including the Internet. In fact, we believe the portal will create an intimacy and loyalty with our customer base that goes beyond anything we've seen before.

We predict that within two years, the portal will be the most important, least noticeable technology within the firm. It is not that difficult to recall a time without PCs, networks, Palm Pilots, cell phones, and the Internet. Now it is difficult to figure out how we lived without all of these. We believe the portal will quickly enter the pantheon of indispensable, life-changing technologies.

Yes, technology is hard to get right, and cultural change is hard to get right. But we see companies getting better at it all the time. Companies that stick with these efforts, especially with the advent of corporate portals, will have a definite competitive advantage. Reaching the Land of Oz is not a fantasy, and we believe PwC will be one of the biggest beneficiaries of these trends.

GOVERNANCE: EVERYONE IS A PUBLISHING COMPANY

Lanes has concluded that the most important issue to address quickly is *governance*. How will the portal be managed? Lanes estimates she spends a full two-thirds of her time on governance and program management issues, with the other third devoted to technology.

Business-to-everything governance in any organization is difficult because it must cut across multiple business units and functions. In a firm like PwC, however, governance of a global technology implementation is akin to navigating grade-five white-water rapids in a swollen river. Without tremendous willpower, it is virtually impossible to get all boats heading in the same direction.

Despite this, the fundamentals of governance are the same. When PwC started its own effort to create the PwC portal, it implemented a structure that is both reactive to a broad and diverse set of stakeholders, while also being lean and responsive to conditions that are necessary for successful transformation programs.

The portal program has a sponsor on PwC's executive board. It has the portal steering committee, made up of business and IT leaders. It has a robust program management office that manages not only the core portal development efforts, but also provides integration management to related infrastructure programs that fall outside of the program's scope.

The first realization was to let go of most issues that had to do with global control. Global control is out, local control is in. Indeed, by 2001, the portal was one of the few global projects under way at PwC. Thus, the portal must be incredibly flexible and act in some ways as a utility. We are trying to remain as geographically neutral as possible and build a portal that is actually decentralized in its operations, governance, and management whenever possible. (There is some centralization around overall strategy of the portal and technology standards, for example.) The benefit of that philosophy is that you end up with decisions, applications, and content originated by people who are much closer to the portal's end users.

Thus, if we find there is no value created by coming together, we won't come together. However, we are also clear that a portal without some central governance will never be built. And if you decline to take advantage of economies of scale, you sell yourself short.

For example, global value is found in the following:

→ *Security.*   It is far better to have 1 logon than 50.

→ *Search engines.*   While both partial and global search capabilities provide value, often, global may be preferred.

→ *Transaction and payment systems.*   Again, a single system is far more efficient than multiple offerings.

With a streamlined core infrastructure, you can decentralize everything else.

In our charter, we laid out 10 components—technologies, structures, content, and management processes—that must be created centrally. The list includes:

1. *Authentication.*   Verifying users' identities when they come to the portal.
2. *Authorization.*   Giving users permission to access applications and content.
3. *Aggregation and enablement of applications and content.*   A single point of access and session management.
4. *Firm-driven profiling.*   Information presented that is based on role or other information we have about the user.
5. *User-driven personalization.*   Individuals structure their views of the site to meet their needs and preferences.
6. *Search.*   Ability to find relevant material.
7. *Content delivery.*   Easy access to timely, relevant information with intuitive navigation.
8. *Collaboration.*   The ability to question, collaborate, and share information with other users.
9. *Payment processing.*   The ability to conduct business, such as purchasing a subscription to a PwC service.
10. *Metrics/reporting.*   Monitoring and measuring usage and operating performance.

As Lanes points out, these functions form the basic core of the system. Beyond that, the portal is like a publishing empire made up of dozens of local newspapers. A general manager will oversee the entire operation, but as in any large publishing company, the editors of the individual publications will decide on the content. The partners in charge of the various lines of business, much like the editors of each newspaper, have significant freedom to implement an application that suits the needs of their users.

To achieve this media company magic, we've learned that you cannot underestimate the need for communications about the portal. The organization must spend a great deal of time getting people on board with what you are doing. For example, we've begun a portal newsletter that circulates online throughout the firm and gives people an update on every aspect of the portal's development.

In this manner, we try to achieve complete transparency. The more people know, the better . . . despite the ever-present voices you'll hear to the contrary. We find that half the problems encountered in the B2E quest is when people don't know what is going on.

Another crucial lesson is to prevent too much bureaucracy and process from impeding the progress. This has been especially difficult for us because the very nature of the firm, as we serve an extremely diverse and varied client base, is to try get everything right for everyone. You simply can't do that in building the portal in the current environment. It will take far too many years.

Ken Cooke, one of the portal builders from the TLS business, says, "We tend to be the classic perfectionist. If you think about our values, we believe in partnership, teamwork, inclusiveness. Those are all very important things and have made us the strong firm we are today. Yet, when you try to build something like the portal across all these constituencies and try to carry your values to the extreme, it will slow your progress." That is exactly why the governance body of the portal must be trusted by all the constituencies to come up with the right answers for the group as a whole.

What makes the PwC portal compelling is that it will

need to be as fluid and flexible as the organization it serves. The question of centralized versus decentralized has plagued the IT world for the past two decades without resolution. Certainly, a portal like HP's or Ford's that can provide a single message from the CEO each morning has tremendous benefits. Central control is faster and more consistent. On the other hand, decentralized may just be how the world works. It is certainly how we work inside PwC.

Obviously, this level of freedom can lead to a disjointed user experience unless strict guidelines are followed. Yet, PwC is going out on many limbs to test the strength and viability of the portal. For example, few corporate portals are multilingual, relying on English, regardless of location. But because of its global nature, PwC is building a multilingual site that offers applications in the language of each office around the world. "There's no right answer on language," Lanes says, "But we feel we have to be multilingual."

And from the outset, Lanes and the other portal planners understood the need to develop a B2E portal, a system that reaches both internal and external users. "The content we have as a knowledge-based organization is just as important to an external audience as to our internal audience," she points out. DiPiazza corroborates that B2E is inherently a collaborative effort. "It is how work gets done," he said, "and it will reshape how we relate to our clients, our colleagues, our alliance partners, outsourced agents, and the business communities we serve."

Of course, we remain a good way from our final destination on the portal implementation. As we have pointed out from the beginning of this book, the portal is a journey, an ever-shifting landscape that will take years to fully coalesce. But as consultants, we are pragmatists and realists. Like our other clients, PwC wants a payoff, sooner rather than later.

In the long run, we believe that the portal will have a dramatic impact on the bottom line, potentially doubling or even tripling revenue per employee. Our size gives us a breadth and depth of resources that competitors can only dream about. But if we are simply bigger and can't match the nimbleness and flexibility of our smaller competitors, then our size becomes a burden. If, however, we can use the portal to connect all of our communities of stakeholders together quickly, efficiently, and globally, then we'll have created something so powerful that it will transform us forever.

CHAPTER SIX

The British Broadcasting Corporation

The British Empire may be a thing of the past, but even today, the sun never sets on the British Broadcasting Corporation (BBC), a communications empire like no other in the world.

The BBC was created in 1922 and has grown into a global broadcast giant with 14 analog and digital television channels, 6 national and 40 local radio channels, and a vast global television production business. In addition, the BBC World Service broadcasts to 153 million radio listeners in 43 languages around the world, reaching across every time zone and every continent to 120 capital cities and across entire nations, including the United States. Not surprising, the BBC is a large, amorphous organization with more than 24,000 full-time employees and another 10,000 regular freelance contractors, such as directors, writers, photographers, and reporters. With its state charter, the BBC is supported in the United Kingdom almost entirely with license fees paid by the public, which generates £2,371,000,000. Its main commercial arm,

BBC Worldwide, a wholly owned subsidiary that sells its television productions, along with a plethora of other publishing offerings and branded properties, generates another £961 million in income for the BBC.

Just as PricewaterhouseCooper's (PwC's) core product is knowledge, the BBC sells creativity. The BBC has produced and exported some of the world's finest television programming, including *Fawlty Towers, Monty Python's Flying Circus,* and more recently, *Madame Bovary, Blue Planet, Teletubbies,* and *Walking with Dinosaurs.* It has a distinguished history of producing high-quality drama, comedy, and educational programming in both television and radio. *The Archers,* for example, began in 1951 as an experimental radio drama aimed at Britain's farmers. It has been on the air for 50 years and reaches 4.9 million listeners every week. Its news operations have been a model for broadcasters around the world. The BBC World Service is known for its unparalleled, in-depth coverage of news and world events. Well before there was CNN on television, the BBC kept the world informed. During World War II, its radio broadcasts sent out coded messages for French Resistance fighters. In 1991, Mikhail Gorbachev tuned in from his Crimean dacha to keep track of the coup in Moscow. Nelson Mandela listened while he was imprisoned in South Africa.

In recent years, the BBC has launched ambitious efforts on the Internet with the highly regarded BBC-i, the most visited content-based online site in Europe, and in state-of-the-art digital broadcasting technology.

Needless to say, the very nature of the BBC differs dramatically from that of a typical manufacturing company. Creating an endless stream of new and innovative programming requires a special kind of mind-set. "Instead of making one thing many times, we make many things once . . . and with passion," says David Scott-Cowan, communications manager of the BBC's SAP Business Center. One doesn't manufacture creativity, creativity happens; economies of scale can be difficult to achieve when each of the products is a one-off. "We, as an organization, tend to resist standardization," says Peter White, Director of Financial Operations for the BBC. "We resist because of the creative culture that we allow to flourish, which makes people believe that every part of their life can be independent."

Managing such a diverse organization, however, requires some standardization, especially in the back office, where costs are captured and annual forecasts and budgets are created and managed. Over the years, the BBC had grown into a large, devolved organization that is supported by many different finance and business systems. By the 1990s, these systems, some of which had been in place for decades, had grown archaic. Islands of technology had grown up everywhere supporting more than 190 autonomous business units with disparate systems that make the sharing of information nearly impossible.

Sir John (now Lord) Birt, the BBC's director-general from 1993 to 2000, embarked on an ambitious program to take the BBC into the digital age, which included the world's first digital radio service in 1995 and, more recently, the launch of a wide range of digital television and Internet services. To support these new initiatives, Birt recognized the need for common business processes and systems across the BBC. It was under his authority that the decision was made to move to a common business-and-finance system, replacing the dozens of local systems then in place and effectively "digitizing the back office." When Greg Dyke, the new director-general, took over the BBC in 2000, he made it clear that vast changes were in order. His goal: to build *one BBC*. To that end, he simplified the divisional structure, making it flatter and less hierarchical. He radically remade the Executive Committee, the board of management that oversees the BBC, adding more representatives from the creative side of the BBC to contribute to the management discussion.

"Our aim is for the BBC to be a place where people work collaboratively, enjoy their job and are inspired and united behind a common purpose—to create great television and radio programs and outstanding online services," Dyke said. "People are proud to work for the BBC, but want to see change. They believe the BBC has taken bold steps towards a strong position in the digital age, but think it has too many managerial layers and costly processes, and that too much time is spent on negotiating within the BBC. As a result, as an organization, we simply move too slowly."

The use of portals and an underlying technology infrastructure that permits an organization-wide sharing of services is a key part of the BBC vision. The idea of "one BBC" does not necessarily mean the creation of a single, enterprise-wide portal connecting all parts of an organization in a seamless system. But it does mean that the movement of work to the web, specifically work on the business side of the organization, could dramatically reduce costs and the endless, time-consuming tasks that have long haunted the BBC's creative talent.

In this way, Dyke and his executive team believe, there will be more time and money aimed at the creation of programs, which is what the business is all about. At the same time, more efficient, integrated systems will also allow the business and financial people to spend far less time tracking mountains of paperwork and take more control of their own tasks. And in this, there are lessons for companies that are coming to depend more and more on innovation to fuel their growth into the future.

Shai Agassi, CEO of SAP Portals, says, "It's all about increased employee productivity. In the 1990s, technology opened up new channels, but left the old channels available for most employees. This did not really change the way most work gets done. B2E starts a new journey. More and more real work will be moved to the web, and companies' productivity will climb. A decade from now, work will look totally different from today, and companies will be far more productive than ever thought possible."

"We will do in the back office what the digital revolution is doing in the front of the house, in television and radio: providing seamless, low cost, easy to access online information," says John Smith, the BBC's director of finance. "It's about giving people information at all levels, immediately, when they want it, as soon as they want it, accurately—and the right kind of information."

In early 2001, Dyke laid out his blueprint for building the BBC of the future. In it, he stated some key goals:

→ To raise the proportion of BBC funding that is spent on programs from 76 to 85 percent by 2005. In 2000, Dyke pointed out, the BBC spent 24 percent of its income on non-program and nonbroadcast costs. That percentage must drop significantly.

→ To create a culture of collaboration, in which people work together for the common purpose of making great programs.

→ To change the way the organization works so that the BBC can make decisions quickly, while retaining sufficient checks and balances to avoid damaging mistakes.

➜ To make sure that the BBC is properly equipped with the skills it needs to compete effectively in the digital world.

➜ To reduce the number of business units from 190 to around 40 and to eliminate the inefficient internal transactions that are so costly and time-consuming.

For an organization as traditional as the BBC, Dyke's mandate was nothing short of revolutionary. But Dyke, whose training came from his years in the competitive world of commercial television, sees no alternative to the massive makeover. Crucially, he threw himself behind the APOLLO campaign, the project (begun under Lord Birt) dedicated to reengineering the BBC's many business processes. The impact of this project on the creative community would be profound. "People will have to learn new ways of working," Dyke stated simply but directly.

GETTING STARTED: THE APOLLO CAMPAIGN

The BBC's embrace of e-business and portals, not surprisingly, has been one of fits and starts. As recently as 1997, the BBC was woefully trailing the digital revolution on the business side of the organization. Without a common digital desktop, the ability to communicate and share information was embarrassingly difficult. For example, there were 24 different e-mail systems within the BBC, and employees in one building could not send an e-mail to someone in the building next door. Layered on that were 29 old and inefficient management systems for the business and financial side of the BBC.

In most companies, such an environment would be difficult enough to manage. But in the BBC, those problems were magnified by the nature of its business. Producing news and entertainment is a highly unpredictable exercise, more art than science. Producers are constantly up against tight deadlines, and very often it is more important to get the story on the air than it is to worry then and there about the underlying business details. On some assignments, it can be difficult to predict with certainty how many people are needed, how long they will work, and what kind of equipment the job requires.

Thus, something as prosaic as raising a purchase order, issuing an invoice, and making a payment can give rise to problems for the program's accountants. When the invoice arrives from a contractor or supplier, it can vary significantly from the original order. As a result, at the end of the month or fiscal quarter or fiscal year, there can be embarrassing shortfalls in anticipated budgets and increases in costs.

In April 1997, the BBC initiated an attempt at a common financial infrastructure with its APOLLO campaign. But at that time, the internal systems infrastructure was a complex mixture of legacy systems, and a myriad of incompatible applications.

The APOLLO campaign was aimed at about 6,000 users and was designed to provide the BBC with a single integrated finance system and a common set of business processes, using standardized software from SAP, a major ERP management software vendor. It formed a series of interrelated projects, including a Shared Service Center, created in March 1998, to manage the BBC's routine financial transactions.

Considering the BBC's environment at the time, APOLLO's aims were ambitious:

→ To improve the efficiency of financial activities, in order to save money

➜ To improve the quality of financial information, in order to enable better business decisions

The APOLLO campaign officially came to an end in July 2001, with the conclusion of the second wave of implementation of SAP. APOLLO demonstrated graphically how difficult it would be to transform the BBC's culture, yet at the same time it proved how desperately the change was needed. The impact of the change was felt most in areas that traditionally had little experience of working directly onto a finance system—for example, in the production offices, and among middle and senior managers who are required to view and interpret reports and to authorize purchases over certain limits. Previously, these groups would use stand-alone or bespoke (proprietary) software, or work offline (e.g., by signing paper-driven approval forms). But the coding complexity required by an ERP system, the menu structures and the number of screens requiring data entry for even the simplest transaction, all contributed to a feeling that this was a way of working imposed on them by accountants for accountants. Whatever the business case may have said, many people in the creative community perceived the new system as having little to offer them in terms of benefits or savings.

Yet if those benefits identified at the outset of APOLLO were to be realized, it was essential that these communities be brought on board. If they continued to work offline, entering information onto the system either late or inaccurately, or both, many of the benefits offered by capturing information at the source would never materialize.

According to Peter White, resistance to change and wariness of new technology on the business side is endemic to the organization. When APOLLO was launched, White spearheaded the effort to create standard ways of working on a common system. "At the time," he recalls, "people were not enthusiastic for change." Only after painstakingly laying the groundwork around the technology implementation did he slowly win converts.

Enterprise resource planning implementations are known to be complex and hard on novice users. White admits it is difficult as he describes staff meetings in which he hunkers down and listens to complaints for hours. "There was a comment from someone who wrote a very vicious e-mail about SAP, saying, 'How can you possibly take away our current system? It's brilliant and the under-pinner of all of our business. You can't possibly replace it with SAP,' " White says. "Someone on my staff pulled out an e-mail from the same person from four or five years ago when the system he was defending was being installed and he said the same thing then about the old system."

But the BBC knew that the creative community was not against technological and organizational change per se. Many creative people have eagerly embraced new technology related to actual production work. Digital technology has dramatically changed the way that programs are made at the BBC. In addition, BBC professionals embraced the concept of virtual teams before that idea had become mainstream in business. To do what they do so well, BBC producers are adept at assembling teams quickly, bringing together a raft of skills and competencies for a specific project, collaborating, and then dispersing and moving on to the next new thing. But the digitizing of the back office, which requires up-front raising of purchase orders, a formal approval process using workflow technology, and a reliance on information derived from the main finance system rather than stand-alone spreadsheets, was seen as additional work that benefited only other people. And since a central plank of the benefits case was a reduction in the headcount of pure finance personnel, it was easy to accuse the implementers of the new system of adding to the workload of already overstretched production teams. A response from a new user, published in the BBC's intranet discussion area, conveys the overall sentiment at the time: "It seems to me that we are taking away resources from making programs in order to become accountants."[1] Moreover, the standardization of ways of working (essential to any ERP implementation) was perceived by some as being profoundly *counterculture*. The BBC is therefore a strange dichotomy, both embracing and disdaining the advent of new technologies, depending on the application.

BUILDING ON SUCCESS: THE BUSINESS PORTAL
It is against this background that the BBC is pioneering the use of SAP portals. As early as 1998, the BBC had a potent taste of B2E with the advent of the Electronic News Production System (ENPS), an early portal built in collaboration with the Associated Press for BBC journalists. Essentially, ENPS is the biggest broadcast newsroom system in the world, with more than 12,000 users in the BBC, tying into 6,500 devices in 300 different locations. "ENPS is the spine of the BBC's daily news production across 12 radio and TV networks, and the Internet," said Richard Sambrook, Director of BBC News. "Without it we would not be as effective or competitive."

The ENPS incorporates nearly everything that journalists need to do their work, including tracking thousands of words of text, hundreds of hours of audio and video pouring in and out of the BBC every day. From the 24-hour news factories in London to the smallest regional radio station, to far-flung foreign correspondents with laptops and modems, the ENPS has become a journalistic lifeline. It feeds online operations and helps the World Service broadcast in 43 languages.

By moving news production to electronic systems in this fashion, the BBC got an early sampling of how portal-type technology could transform the way people work. But the ENPS is, in effect, an island of technology, aimed at its target audience without plans to integrate it with other BBC systems.

So the lessons here were double-edged: If you build a portal in total isolation, its focus is likely to be too narrow and offer limited objectives. It might even create more work. Building a single organizational portal, however, even one that simply connects hundreds of independent portals, can be transformational. It requires an organization that is ready for such a dramatic makeover. At the BBC, such a makeover is no simple task.

Flash forward to October 2001, and the BBC launched the pilot for its SAP enterprise portal for the financial and business side of the organization. While the BBC management is absolutely committed to this massive changeover, it comes on the heels of APOLLO, which produced great frustration and pain among its 6,000 users.

White, who has suffered the slings and arrows of leading the APOLLO effort, has come to understand the nature of the beast. After a dozen years in the television business, the last nine at the BBC, he is undeterred by resistance. He refuses to bow to the creativity argument, even while acknowledging the brilliance of the creative process within the BBC. To make certain that he is not distracted by the noisy feedback, he has imposed his own version of loose/tight management for the implementation of the portal. The changes, he says, must be imposed because they otherwise will not be willingly accepted. But at the same time, he tells people they don't have to use the portal if they don't want to. His belief, based on smaller but similar implementations over the past few years, is that eventually the BBC portal will be embraced.

For the portal, Peter White wants to combine the benefits of streamlined processes and a unified corporate voice. "There have always been lots of different business processes allowed to flourish in their own way," he says, "and therefore it was difficult to communicate what the standard process was. The old expense policy, for example, said, 'Your expenses must be submitted within six weeks of return from your travel. If they are not returned within six weeks, then they must be returned within three months.' That gives an idea of how it's been here. Nobody knows what the rules are. So for me, this is about knowing there is a very clear distinction between the creative process, what's created, and just doing good business. This is about communicating key processes and getting the business of this organization working properly in the background."

The SAP portal is part of the foundation for the BBC's ambitious effort to create a set of common standards for a series of financial transactions that are key to the company's business. The total target audience for the business portal numbers 4,500 BBC workers. It is being rolled out very slowly, though, starting with 50 targeted users in 2001 (with another 50 involved in user acceptance testing), and the plan is to roll it out at a rate of 100 to 200 people per month, providing a user base of 500 by April 2002. At that point, further plans for the rollout will be finalized.

Working with SAP, along with Medas (a joint venture between PwC and EDS), the BBC is moving away from these fragmented technologies into a single common set of financial and HR applications. The first step is to provide back-office purchasing information onto senior managers' desktops with a simple, user-friendly interface, anytime they need it. In this manner, the key community will feel as if the new system is being offered, not thrust at them.

"Our vision is a portal for every BBC employee which provides relevant, useful information specific to each individual's role," White said. "Bringing purchasing authorization online is the first crucial step in this process."

For White, confidence in the new portal comes from the fact that its foundation is the world wide web. "More and more people, including myself, are doing everything online," White says. "I do my personal banking, my shopping. So culturally, people want to go to the web. They are not resistant to it. And once you've got them using the portal, you can then start building things in the portal that drive processes that are harder to capture. You get rid of uncertainty and clunking around different systems."

THE IMPORTANCE OF THE CEO

As Hewlett-Packard, Ford, and PwC have also learned, gaining widespread acceptance is difficult and crucial. There is no force more potent in gaining this acceptance than the CEO. Like Fiorina at HP, Greg Dyke at the BBC understood the importance of the B2E revolution from the outset and became a visible and vocal supporter of the effort.

Indeed, when Dyke came on board, he encountered a maelstrom. According to White, Dyke could have shut down the SAP implementation as part of a moratorium he imposed on various projects at the time. Instead, after enduring countless meetings and raging battles about whether to proceed or stop, Dyke said, "We need to do this and I need to lead it." He created a steering committee and named himself as its chairman. His message to the staff: "It will be a pain, but please bear with it and help where you can—we do need it."

Scott-Cowan echoes White in his belief that top management has to get behind an SAP implementation project if it is to have a chance. In the past, top-level commitment to such projects has varied and left mixed messages with the BBC population. "Things started to move very fast when Greg came in because he saw this as being an enabler of his vision of one BBC," Scott-Cowan said. "He sees this as something that can help release more money for program making, and put the creative people back at the heart of the BBC."

Not a technologist, Dyke stepped back from the process once it got rolling. He had other fish to fry. But as White pointed out, "He was critical to its success." In fact, a staff survey taken three months after the final SAP implementation provided clear evidence that most people understood why the effort was being made and that it was something the BBC had to do. "I'm very clear why," White said. "It's because Greg said we have to do it."

Once Dyke threw down the gauntlet, the next phase was to grease the wheels of acceptance. At the BBC, usability has been a key issue, particularly as the standard SAP has been introduced to some executive producers and senior producers on the creative side. The portal was seen as a way of enabling them to work effectively with the system in a more intuitive way. But White was not in favor of changing something as fundamental as the look and feel of the new system for all users so soon after implementation. Starting with a small target group was the preferred route. Rather than roll the system out to all 4,500 targeted users at once, the BBC and the consultants agreed to identify 50 key users and turn them into the pioneers.

The purpose of bringing these particular users into the equation is that they are the influencers, the ones who must sign off on all purchase orders. In the old manual system, invoices could get tracked all over the BBC and often sit unattended on producers' desks while suppliers waited interminably to get paid. To get these occasional users to use the SAP system, White and his staff had to convince them of the benefits of the portal. The idea was simple but powerful: These may be infrequent users, but they are very influential users. If you can get them on board, the rest will follow.

So with that in mind, White's team focused on the presentation of the portal. Television producers, for example, pay attention to what things look like, the style and design. It had to *look* BBC, and it had to *feel* BBC. Being empathetic to the culture is a key lesson in portal implementation.

PUSHING PEOPLE'S MINDS TOWARD THE POSSIBLE

True to the environment, White and his team are not content to simply roll out the portal for the business side and walk away. He envisions the portal as just a first step to expansive and exciting potential. "Portal technology enables you to do things you never dreamed of being able to do," White said. "It's important to keep on pushing people's minds about what is possible. It would be so boring for me if this was about sorting last year's business process problems. This is about, how can we be really different; how can we challenge people to keep thinking about what can be done?"

To that end, White intends to introduce new ideas, ideas generated by BBC staff themselves, onto the portal every two or three months. They don't have to be massive projects or enhancements, but processes made possible by the Internet that weren't possible before. Ironically, part of the education process in implementing a portal is explaining to people that the portal itself does not arrive loaded with content. The content—things like webcams, weather updates—is available at the BBC and will be integrated into the portal environment over time.

Whether the BBC ultimately chooses a single portal for the entire organization remains unknown at this point. According to White, it is highly unlikely. He cannot envision journalists in search of stories and research material using the SAP system for such work. However, he does foresee the advent of a single business portal, which may well be built upon the SAP portal. Like other big companies, the BBC is enthusiastic about employee self-service in areas such as HR, which will likely become a vast B2E opportunity.

Just as companies like HP, Ford, and PwC are in the early stages of portal development, the BBC's overarching issue is connecting up all of the people inside the BBC in a way that takes full advantage of the web. There are countless opportunities to draw people together.

Scott-Cowan points out that the BBC is reviewing all of its business processes—purchasing, internal resources, the way the vast freelance community is managed, hiring actors—to find extensions to the portal. Part of the purpose of this is to promote shared knowledge of the way things are done in the business. "We've always had to relearn and relearn things," Scott-Cowan said. "Things got done by the will of the people, but there was little shared knowledge of how the place worked. It was very difficult."

THE ART OF TRANSFORMATION

Finding ways to capture corporate knowledge and make it accessible to everyone will ultimately be the most dramatic change fueled by the B2E push. For example, a survey of the BBC's production offices not long ago revealed that the most time-consuming process was finding an audio, video, or film clip from the BBC's own archives. With more than 50 years' worth of material filling several warehouses, the task was ponderous at best. The entire collection was card-indexed. A producer seeking a certain clip had to call the archives, describe what he or she wanted, and sit back and wait. In the archives, a researcher had to search through the card index and hope that what they discovered was either exactly or close to what had been requested.

They would spool through the tape or film, sometimes all the way to the end, to make sure it was the right clip and then copy it to video- or audiotape and send it over by courier. Once received, the producer had to view the material and if it was indeed what he or she wanted, the next step was to pore over a list of requirements such as who owned the rights, if there were third-party costs, coproduction credits, and how permission for use could be gotten. Documentation had to be manually drawn up before a clip could actually be used in a program. After all that, the producer still had to go back to the master tape and get a transmission-quality copy of the little bit they wanted to use, which meant booking very expensive equipment and people's time. Only then could the final bit be edited into the program.

"Not surprisingly, some people actually found it cheaper and easier to go out and reshoot the material," Scott-Cowan said. "Because even after the entire process, you weren't absolutely sure that you were getting the best clip out there."

Digitizing all the material in the archives will transform the entire process. And with a portal not unlike the ENPS system, clips will be e-mailed online from the archive, eventually perhaps directly into a production unit's digital editing system. A scan of the rights database could resolve all the paperwork in minutes, and the transfer of this vital information would be done in minutes rather than days or weeks.

By integrating the organization's systems, a producer who accepts the archive clip will, with a click of the mouse, seamlessly set in motion the purchase order for the clip in the SAP portal. Like current retail web sites, a drop of some product into the digital shopping basket automatically creates a purchase order. In this way, the creative people, just by doing their jobs, will fulfill the administrative tasks running in the background without any unnecessary input and time required from them.

Integrating a preferred suppliers list into the BBC's purchasing environment is yet another potentially powerful and cost-saving application. With over 30,000 suppliers across the BBC and few enforceable rules to limit where one purchases supplies, the organization has left some leverage by the door and savings on the table. The BBC buys an enormous supply of videotape, for example, and currently there is no enforced policy requiring people to buy from certain suppliers.

With the SAP portal, a preferred supplier list could be whittled down to four suppliers. A purchaser would need only to click on videotape, and the list would pop on screen. An e-mail link would allow queries to be made about inventory and delivery times. By settling on a limited list of preferred suppliers, an organization as vast as the BBC could use its leverage to receive pricing breaks that will result in significant cost savings over time.

For White and Scott-Cowan, these scenarios embody their philosophy in a vivid way. Scott-Cowan, a former producer himself, decided to leave the creative side and work on the APOLLO campaign and, later, the portal effort because he saw the gulf at the BBC widening between the creative and business sides of the organization. "I've always said that the good financing of programs is as much a part of the creative process as good scriptwriting and good editing," he said. "The more control you have up front of the way you are managing those finances, the better that program stands to be and the less mess you'll have waiting for you at the end of the project."

As this attitude seeps into the BBC's culture, the obvious benefits will be on the bottom line. "On the business side, the only reason we're doing this is to save money," White said. He noted that the £50 million in annual savings will likely be split between the finance and purchasing departments. Detailed savings plans are in place in each division.

White has planned out the implementation like a chess match, moving pieces into place in some parts of the organization, leaving others as they were . . . for now. The early implementation of a new expense system, called e-expenses, was targeted at 60 percent of the BBC population. "I wanted to deliver something in an appropriate timescale," White said. "I knew we'd never get agreement from the other forty percent. The savings was to be had in that sixty percent anyway."

Another factor impacting the rollout is that the BBC has long been a bastion of free speech and open debate. "We don't shut down noise, we allow it to flourish," White explained. Dissenting letters are regularly printed in the staff newsletter. While in the middle of the two phases of the SAP rollout in late 2000, White felt particularly vulnerable. After the first wave of 3,000 users was hooked into the SAP desktop, a massive revolt could have shut things down even before the second wave was brought in. It required a period of conciliatory behavior on White's part, but it eventually worked.

This kind of delicate but strong-willed direction is crucial within the BBC. Technology implementations across the entire organization require the flexibility to include local variations where necessary, not unlike the PwC model.

In the end, White echoes the famed Nike ad when he offers up the lessons he's learned over the past several years. "When it comes to an ERP implementation, *just do it*," he declared. "One of the worst things is to stand around and pontificate and not do what is hard."

At the same time, he adds, it is crucial to make sure people understand why the transformation is taking place. Barking orders without explanations will never fly in an organization filled with creative and talented people.

Last of all, you must listen to the people's reactions, both the good and the bad. "Our people sometimes find it hard going out to talk to the users who are going to give them a hard time," White said. "We do a lot of that. I don't like it. But it is very important to do because this might be their only opportunity to talk about how awful it is. So it's important not to shut yourself away, however strong the temptation."

Though it is difficult to forecast what the BBC might look like in the next few years due to its current transformation, the paths that are being opened are numerous. Using the power of digital communication and the remarkable reach of the Internet, an organization as vast as the BBC will gain greater flexibility and save significant amounts of money by tying together the organization via portals. Scott-Cowan sees this happening even in the creative process, where managers will realize that it doesn't matter whether somebody is doing the job at their kitchen table or an office in London.

"Teams will come together when they really need to be together, when they really need face-to-face communication," he said. "But there could be far more time spent online in disparate places."

More than that, the portal will expand in ways that have only been imagined thus far. The ability to manage projects and garner rights approvals as the BBC grows and exploits the third-party use of its products will make the portal a powerful and profitable tool. In the best of all possible worlds, the backbreaking implementation of technology will eventually become invisible, integrated seamlessly into an environment that is focused solely on producing an endless supply of exquisite programming.

"The creative side of program making comes essentially from the whole person, not a computer system, and that will never change," Scott-Cowan said. "Really good programs come from the heart and that's as it should be. What we can do is enable those people to spend their time where they are working best, in a creative environment, and make the administrative side as easy for them as possible."

CHAPTER SEVEN
Leadership

For the leader, the scenery is always changing. Everything is new.
—Warren Bennis[1]

The September 11 terrorist attacks in New York City and Washington, D.C., changed the world in many ways. The scope of this tragedy touched every life in our nation. That day, so stunning and horrific, tested even the toughest, most effective leaders in every company, small and large.

In our firm, with its complex organizational structure and lack of a centralized command and control hierarchy, the opportunity for chaos and confusion on such a cataclysmic day was significant. Like many other big firms, PricewaterhouseCoopers suffered personally. We tragically lost five people who were on flights that crashed that day.

As that terrible day unfolded, Sam DiPiazza, then territory senior partner in charge of the United States, sent a series of messages to all U.S. partners and employees. Here are a few of those messages:

Samuel A. DiPiazza Jr.
09/11/2001 10:41 AM
To: People of PwC

As you are aware, we are facing a national emergency due to the terrorist attacks in New York and Washington, DC this morning. Our leadership in New York is attempting to determine if we had any people in the World Trade Center Towers or on either of the two aircraft. At this point we have nothing to report.

Our people should remain calm and follow the direction of our Office Managing Partners. We are closely monitoring the developments.

Words are not adequate at a time like this. I know, however, that we all feel the impact of this terrible act and we all feel like victims. My thoughts and prayers are with those who have been injured and with their families.

Sam

Samuel A. DiPiazza Jr.
09/11/2001 04:13 PM
To: People of PwC

I am writing to ask for your help in two areas. First, as a result of today's airport shutdowns across the country, many of our people are stranded away from home with few hotel rooms available in the major cities.

If you are a stranded PwC traveler and need a hotel room for tonight please contact American Express Travel at the phone number you normally use. AmEx is negotiating for blocks of rooms wherever available, and will be open until 2:00 a.m. tomorrow morning to assist you. You can also contact a PwC volunteer host. Click on the link below for a list of volunteer hosts.

If you can serve as a PwC volunteer host and offer an extra room in your home, we are requesting your assistance. If you are able to accommodate a PwC guest for tonight, please click on the link below . . . and enter your name, address, and contact numbers. If a traveler calls you and arranges to stay with you overnight, please update your listing in the database to say "unavailable." Thank you in advance for pitching in to help a PwC colleague.

Another important request: Please consider donating blood because it will be needed. While we do not yet know the number, we do know that many hundreds of people have been injured in the terrorist attacks. Contact your local American Red Cross office, or check on local TV stations for locations near you.

PwC people across the country, and from around the world, are reaching out to help each other. Thank you for caring so much and please keep our people and our country in your prayers.

Sam

Samuel A. DiPiazza Jr.
09/11/2001 04:42 PM
To: People of PwC

I know each of you are concerned about whether PwC people could have been caught up in today's senseless acts which have stunned our nation.

Since early this morning we have had teams working frantically to locate our partners and staff members who where either traveling today or were working with clients in the World Trade Center area of lower Manhattan. We do not have any PwC offices in that part of New York. The teams have been contacting engagement teams and

Office Managing Partners around the country to pinpoint everyone's location.

We can report that almost all of our people are safe but we will not stop working until we have accounted for all of them. We are all praying that everyone returns home safely.

Sam

Samuel A. DiPiazza Jr.
09/12/2001 10:41 AM
To: People of PwC

Yesterday afternoon, I asked for your assistance in reaching out to the PwC people who were stranded in cities around the country, particularly in the New York area. Your response was overwhelming. Within 13 minutes of my note, 274 of you had volunteered your homes as a refuge. By the end of the day, 2,021 volunteer hosts had entered their names into the database.

Sometimes we think that our Firm is so large that we are not connected to each other. This is not true. When the chips were down, PwC people stepped forward and reached out to their colleagues—even though they did not know their names or faces. And there were more blood donors than we can even begin to count.

I want to thank each one of you who opened your hearts and doors to our extended PwC family and to the victims of the disaster. You make me very proud to be part of this fine and strong firm.

Sam

Samuel A. DiPiazza Jr.
09/12/2001 02:11 PM

To: People of PwC

I am very sorry to tell you that we now have confirmed the loss of the five PwC people mentioned in my note earlier this morning. They were all passengers on the aircraft involved in yesterday's crashes. Three of the victims were on our ABAS staff, one was an MCS partner, and one was a TLS partner. It is difficult to write this, but I want you all to know about these colleagues whose senseless deaths turn a national tragedy into personal loss for every one of us in PwC.

[DiPiazza then mentioned each of the departed, described their professional and educational background, and by whom they were survived.]

These professionals stood for everything good about this Firm. Their dedication to their colleagues and to their families was obvious to everyone they touched. Words simply cannot express the sadness I feel at this moment.

We are still in the process of tracking down all the PwC people who may have been in the World Trade Center area working on client engagements. Our teams in New York have been directly in touch with thousands of our staff. At this point, I do not have anything more to report but will be back to you as soon as we have confirmed that all of our people are safe.

As the day goes on, I learn that more and more of our PwC people have lost family members and friends in the catastrophe. Please pray for the families, friends, and loved ones of [our dearly departed,] and please pray for the many PwC people who are suffering grief and an overwhelming sense of loss.

Sam

Samuel A. DiPiazza Jr.
09/25/2001 04:42 PM
To: People of PwC

It is very difficult to describe the emotions we have each felt in the fourteen days since September 11th. The images of the devastation at the Pentagon and the World Trade Center are forever embedded in our memories. These images, and the emotions they create, will stay with us for a long time to come.

On Sunday, my wife, Melody, and I took a walk in our neighborhood and visited NYC Fire Department, Engine Company 22, on East 85th Street. We have walked past this small station dozens of times and felt the comfort of knowing that New York's bravest were at work. This company lost nine of its own that terrible Tuesday morning.

While this news deepened our sense of loss, the resolve of these firefighters to rebuild their team along with the tremendous support they are receiving from the community has enhanced my own appreciation of the human spirit. Yes, we have all suffered an incalculable loss but we have an enormous capacity to recover.

It struck me that our own Firm has been exhibiting this same resolve and spirit. I have watched our people give their hearts and souls to the families of our lost colleagues.

You have responded in an enormous way to our PwC "People who Care" effort. You have submitted over 1,000 notes of support to the families of our lost colleagues. And your financial support has been equally impressive. (I will be updating you on the PwC People who Care Foundation in a week or so). In case you need the link to the database it is included below for your convenience.

Like Engine Company 22 here in Manhattan—our spirit

burns brighter than ever. PricewaterhouseCoopers has come together through this crisis and, as one team, as one family, we will emerge stronger. We each need to translate the strong sense of team we have found in the last two weeks to our everyday interactions with each other and our clients. And we will begin to regain a sense of normalcy in our business.

In the next few days I will issue another memo about gradually getting back to business and our intentions regarding travel. I hope you will find my guidelines to be both sensitive to your safety and concerns while respecting that we have clients to serve and livelihoods to protect.

We have experienced two weeks of pain and sorrow. Now, it is our responsibility to our lost friends and colleagues—and to our country—to stare this enemy in the face and reclaim our future. You have made me proud over these tough two weeks. I know you will continue to do so as we move towards our future.

Sam

NEW STYLES OF LEADERSHIP

There is no way to overstate the impact and importance of Sam's communication to the firm during that tumultuous time. Sam's calm, reassuring voice echoed throughout our vast and geographically dispersed company. In the PwC environment, where so many of us are regularly out on the road visiting clients or working from home or hotel rooms, very few people get to know the firm's leaders personally.

When the crisis occurred, Sam embraced technology as the perfect medium to deliver his all-important messages to everyone, instantly, around the country and the world. Through him, we knew what was happening inside the firm. We received updates on travel policies, safety concerns, and these personal messages that brought us together in a way that we had never been before. We felt we knew Sam. We established a relationship in those grim days, a strong connection that carried enormous influence when it was most needed.

Sam didn't realize it at the time, but the portal changed his style and effectiveness as a leader. It made a huge difference in his ability to take charge in a truly shocking situation and pull our forces together to get through the crisis. And one more significant thing happened: Within weeks of the terrible event, PwC's partners voted to make Sam DiPiazza the firm's new CEO. As you have read in the preceding case studies, everything is indeed new, especially when it comes to leading the B2E effort. Like any significant organizational transformation, moving a company into the world of B2E requires a different mind-set, along with a new set of metrics by which to measure success. September 11 was a dramatic and graphic sample of this transformation, but changes had already begun to take shape well before the tragedy.

As evidenced by Carly Fiorina, Sam DiPiazza, Greg Dyke, Tom Siebel, Jacques Nasser, and the other leaders who have already embarked on a B2E path, these kinds of changes are not subtle and definitely not easy. There is great risk involved when one sets in motion something as cataclysmic as changing the way work is done. Bringing together a thousand tribes requires new leadership metrics—a new way to think about the organization and how to move it forward.

"I see the CEO's job, not as a maximizer of shareholder value, profitability, and growth," says Siebel. "The CEO's job is really to be the source of and communicator of the corporate culture that holds the organization together. In order to do this, he or she must communicate directly with every employee every day."

While one cannot create an effective leader from a single mold, we believe there are several key characteristics that leaders in the new B2E environment must embrace:

→ *They must lead out in the open, not from behind the closed doors of an executive suite.* In a B2E environment, transparency and being out front are crucial.

→ *They are leading **people**, not employees.* The B2E portal allows workers to incorporate their work and personal lives in new, creative ways. Leaders must recognize this new environment and understand that it is both more complex and more liberating to run a B2E organization.

→ *Leadership can be and should be far more personal.* The portal offers a whole new level of two-way communication with the entire company. Leaders who succeed in this environment must embrace that personal relationship and make it part of their daily agenda.

→ *They must not only create the vision for the future, they must show how to get there.* Moving work to the web is a transformative experience. A strong leader has to literally lead the way.

Though some leaders believe that difficult economic cycles are the best time to make these changes, there is always the chance that such economic forces will undermine the effort itself. Often, in the Darwinian world of business, a leader will be forced out by the board before he or she can complete the task, as happened to Nasser at Ford.

In reality, corporate leadership has been undergoing dramatic changes for the past decade or more, so the B2E revolution is unlikely to catch many CEOs steeped in ignorant bliss or isolated in an ivory tower. As companies have become global, workforces more diverse, and technology has spawned dramatic changes in work processes, leaders have been confronted by the stark clarity that things aren't as they used to be.

That epiphany, however, provides little guidance for corporate leaders who are faced with the inevitable shifts that are underway, knowing it doesn't necessarily offer up the solution for how to lead through it. One thing about which we are certain, the winners will emerge from those who are proactive, rather than reactive, to this new environment. A successful B2E implementation requires a leader who is willing to double-down when the odds seem stacked against the plan.

We also believe that this is not a technology initiative that can be handed off to the IT department or delegated down through layers of bureaucracy.

There is an open debate about whether leadership can be taught at all. We are fascinated by that discussion, but we won't take up the issue here. We assume that most CEOs have demonstrated the requisite leadership skills to have reached their lofty positions in the first place (though we are not naïve enough to believe that every CEO is a successful leader).

The push toward a true B2E environment, however, is going to require leaders to reconsider all of the notions about organizational behavior and structure that they've held for much of their careers. In his best-selling 1989 book, *On Becoming a Leader,* Warren Bennis laid out the key personal and organizational characteristics for coping with change, forging a new future, and creating learning organizations. In the dozen years since the book was published, most of these characteristics have become more crucial than ever.

Effective leaders, Bennis said, will "have the capacity to create a compelling vision, one that takes people to a new place, and then to translate that vision into reality."[2] In a B2E organization, the CEO must create the vision of the new organization and be willing to take the heat as the transition gets underway. As Nasser and Fiorina learned firsthand, the pushback can be tremendous, especially during difficult economic periods.

What's more, Bennis pointed out another truism that impacts B2E implementations: Leaders must *lead,* not *manage.* In the very heart of the B2E environment lies the ability to allow people to manage their own careers and their own lives. By creating strict standards across the B2E portal, the most effective leaders will build a loose/tight structure that provides great freedom and discipline as work is moved to the web.

Bennis penned a long list of differences between the leader and the manager. Several apply directly to the B2E environment:

→ The manager administrates; the leader innovates.

→ The manager focuses on systems and structure; the leader focuses on people.

→ The manager relies on control; the leader inspires trust.

→ The manager has a short-range view; the leader has a long-range perspective.

> ➜ The manager does things right; the leader
> does the right thing.

LEADING OUT IN THE OPEN

The B2E portal presents an opportunity for leaders to
lead in a new way. We call it *leading out in the open.*
Because the portal reaches internal customers (employees)
and outside customers, there is an unprecedented opportunity to open communication channels that never existed
before, channels that allow for connections anytime, anywhere to all levels of the organization.

A leader can now interact with the suppliers of ideas
and products, the creators, as never before in new and
innovative ways—e-mail, webcasts, teleconferences,
chats—and thus take levels of bureaucracy out of the
relationships. And in an economic downturn, when costs
must be carefully controlled, leaders have new opportunities to cut costs without reducing their reach.

In this environment, the leader must be out front,
highly visible, and realize that leadership by memo and
committee will no longer suffice.

To give B2E a chance to be successful, the CEO as
well as the B2E chief must take on broader roles than in
the past. They must become facilitators, coaches, and
advisors and push the concept along. One is hard pressed
to think of a time over the past two decades when CEOs
have gotten out in public forums to discuss IT innovation
at their firms. But now, leaders like Fiorina are regular
speakers at conferences and gatherings, extolling the
virtues of e-business and the positive impact that the
Internet is having on their companies.

With diverse, global workforces, the corporate
landscape is dramatically different. People don't come
to work at the same place every day, and the very

nature of their jobs has shifted in ever-increasing cases. How do you lead a workforce in 50 countries speaking 20 different languages? How do you take on the dichotomy of a more dispersed, virtual workforce that demands more personal contact with its leaders?

CEOs who tour remote corporate outposts once a year can no longer assume such behavior will be adequate and effective. Business to everything actually allows leaders to create a feeling in the minds of most stakeholders of being there everyday. When HP employees log on to @hp, the first thing they see is Fiorina's picture and a new message from her about some aspect of the HP community.

In this way, Fiorina's leadership becomes much more personal. Whether an employee is in Palo Alto or Geneva, they still feel as if they know her and, more important, know what she wants to do. Perhaps even more important, the messages are reaching everyone, unfiltered and unedited. Reaching everyone in the organization with the same message is a hugely impactful event, something unheard of in corporations before the advent of the Internet.

With this tool, Nasser at Ford touched the world-wide Ford community in ways that were once impossible. The impact is impressive. Each employee feels as if the CEO is talking directly to them, and they can respond instantly and say anything. This kind of connection was simply unheard of in the days prior to the advent of the portal. Becoming personal and virtual at the same time is the by-product of the B2E portal.

LEADING THE WAY
As Bennis said, leaders must be able to translate the vision into reality. We've seen time and again leaders who create the vision but aren't able to show the way.

Employees faced with a radically new way to think about work are likely to be skeptical. They'll say, "That sounds great. How do we do it?"

At HP, every employee has been given an *Inventor's Guide,* an actual document that explains how to reinvent your work and move it to the portal. The idea is to deconstruct the work process, think through the structure of the work, and move it to the portal. At the same time, the portal becomes the framework for how one leads the organization—the collaboration, the communication, and the managing of a global workforce.

Hewlett-Packard has also incorporated its portal into its leadership training programs for employees. Prospective managers are asked to consider how to use the capabilities of @hp to increase the power of their leadership. In just a short time, it has become recognized as a tool for increasing leadership skills. This is prescient on HP's part. We believe that everyone in the organization needs to develop these leadership skills to some degree. If we expect employees to manage themselves using the portal, then we must equip them with the skills to communicate, collaborate, and create communities on their own.

At PwC, where we have a widespread, nomadic workforce, the ability to manage distributed and remote offices is crucial to maintaining and strengthening the reality of one global firm. Leadership across the organization is suddenly possible with the portal. In the past, we needed hoards of staff people to provide necessary information in order for decisions to be made. With that kind of information available in a self-service buffet on the portal, employees don't need access to the company jet or backrooms filled with accountants. Not only can we flatten the organization, eliminate the muddled layers of bureaucracy, but all of us can be leaders!

Inside our firm, for example, Kersten Lanes has led the B2E portal effort by insisting on creating a mission statement and getting everyone focused on the same goal. "If you don't know what the scope of the project is, you won't know if you are successful," Lanes says and we agree. Through the portal, she has become a leader, driving the effort globally.

Similarly at Health Net, Inc., Karin Mayhew, the senior vice president of organizational effectiveness, and formerly senior vice president of human resources, played a broad role in making the portal a reality, far beyond the HR function. She was not only the facilitator and process manager for the effort but served as coach and advisor to many others on the project. She pushed the idea along, getting others in the organization to start looking at the portal in a new way. And she managed the change effectively by focusing on the details of preparing for that change, something many organizations don't do well enough.

For CEOs, the portal offers the opportunity to walk out of the ivory tower for good. Tired of and frustrated with the isolation as well as the inability to get their messages through to the troops unfiltered, the B2E portal gives direct access and communication. In that, there is immense power.

While it has already become impossible for a CEO to lead without knowing how to do e-mail, the same type of requirements will soon be in place for the portal. In tomorrow's corporate environment, a CEO will have to learn to embrace and use the power of the portal or his or her tenure will be short-lived.

And like the transition from silent movies to talkies, the portal opens up an entirely new environment that may well be perfect for leaders who otherwise struggled to lead. Some may end up as better leaders over the portal than in person. Some silent film stars could not make the switch into movies with sound. This new technology will undoubtedly lead to a new generation of corporate stars. Some can work in either medium, but some cannot make the transition.

TRANSFORMING EVERYTHING

Bad times require great leaders, whether in war or in business. Today, great leaders require great technology. To build employee confidence in the marketplace and in new ideas, a CEO cannot become less visible. After September 11, most companies had travel bans in place, and most kept to a regimen of much restricted travel for months afterward. With a portal, CEOs had the tool and mechanism to stay visible and influence morale and momentum. E-mail alone or videoconferencing is not enough.

Leadership used to be about meetings. Leaders were raised on meetings. In the B2E world, leadership is no longer about meetings, which is a good thing, because people have come to loathe the endless meetings that hogged their time. For a long time, people have asked, "Why are we having this meeting? How come this couldn't be handled on the web?"

The portal offers a way to collect and disseminate information on a topic and build momentum to make change happen. The art of leadership here becomes less about meetings, more about using the power of technology to collect information and to guide an organization toward its goals. And in a world where travel becomes more suspect, difficult, and costly, the organization of tomorrow will incorporate Alvin Toffler's electronic cottage concept in ways that were only pipedreams in the 1980s. If more and more people want to and need to work at home, either for fear of terrorist attacks or because they have reprioritized their lives, the organization needs to accommodate this desire.

Most companies tried to attend to the personal needs of their employees with varying degrees of success. Despite the best of intentions, some work just didn't lend itself to flex time, work at home, or other experimental working arrangements. September 11 changed all of that dramatically. That personal aspect that couldn't be acknowledged in the United States in a significant business way is much more important now. Employees who want to work at home need access from home. This puts stresses on the systems as never before. It also creates a paradox for organizations: If the new cultural imperative is to be at home more, but business requires even more contact with customers, suppliers, fellow workers, and managers, how will you handle that paradox?

The portal lets people connect without being there. As the technology advances, the portal will offer access to home through broadband connections that will incorporate live video sessions with spouses and children. These connections will work from the office as well. The long-awaited concept of *virtual* may finally become a reality.

Leaders need to recognize these shifts and be prepared to incorporate this new work style into their agendas. The sudden legitimacy of this new emphasis on the inevitable intertwining of work and personal lives forces leaders to view the world in a new way. *You are now leading people, not employees.* Employees were the people who ran accounts payable or managed a product development group from 8 A.M. to 5 P.M. After that, they morphed into something else: parents, spouses, partners, Little League coaches, soccer moms, car poolers, community activists, volunteers, and so forth.

Every person is the leader of their own complex world. The goals of the organization now must align to some degree with the goals and visions that people have for their own worlds. That is only possible with the B2E portal, which bridges the professional and personal sides of a person's life. It provides the connection and the legitimacy of this new relationship with work.

For leaders, dealing with people instead of employees creates a much more complex environment. At the same time, leaders cannot ignore the harsh realities of quarterly earnings and economic cycles. Despite all that has been written about the harshness of downsizing and cost cutting, corporate executives have yet to find a substitute for layoffs during downturns. We wish we could offer an alternative that would solve the problem.

In fact, leaders may have to cut less deeply if they can find a way to harness the power and creative energy of employees and connect up to those who survive the cuts and those who don't. With increased energy to move markets, cuts simply won't have to be as deep. Companies in turmoil are not conducive to gaining market share. There is gossip, strife, and people feel disconnected. Conversely, a company that remains connected via the portal, that knows the vision, that sees products in the pipeline, and that knows how to compete, cannot only survive but rebuild to even greater successes. The portal may not obviate the need for cost cutting, but it may make those cuts sustainable over time.

For companies that are focused only on deep cutting, it is likely that a major artery will be severed and the company will die. New leaders find ways to avoid this by harnessing the power of employees' innovation to channel new ideas through the company. The portal may not eliminate the need for R&D, but it surely makes every employee an inventor.

Some savvy companies have turned to fresh ideas rather than cutbacks. Why not put together a sabbatical program, offer people a percentage of their compensation, give them health benefits, and keep them connected via the portal? When the downturn ends, they will be able to rejoin the company without missing a beat. As expensive as it is to let someone go and even more expensive to bring someone new on board, this concept provides intriguing options.

In truth, we can only speculate as to the power of the portal as it becomes a ubiquitous part of an organization. Options we may not even see today will open up tomorrow due to a melding of technology and new leadership.

As that is happening, CEOs must focus on the crucial role they have in setting and leading the vision. Without that, the B2E revolution will die before it gathers steam. At Ford, for example, Jacques Nasser came under fire and tremendous pressure as the company struggled through the recent recession. Even though he resigned in late 2001 in the midst of harsh economic pressures, Nasser never wavered in his commitment to moving Ford to the Internet. We fully expect his successors to support that commitment as the company attempts to turn its fortunes around.

"We've said that the Internet is the twenty-first-century equivalent of the moving assembly line Ford pioneered in the twentieth century," Nasser said. "We intend to take full advantage of it and be a leader in shaping the future as we did in the past."

Nasser's words would have been empty had he not followed up with a personal commitment to the change. W. James Fish, retired executive director at Ford, points out that Nasser's role in the rollout of B2E was key. "While people are wondering, 'What's the impact of this? What's our role going to be?' if you get a vision from the top that guides people, it is very powerful."

It is also very powerful for the CEO to be able to

bring together a multinational, multilayered organization and reach everyone, from senior levels to plant workers seven layers down in the hierarchy. With the Internet and the portal, leaders have found this gem: the pathway for unfiltered communication that jumps layers of bureaucracy and vast geographies. Because we are so much in the early stages of this new world, we don't know exactly what the art of the possible looks like. But from what we've witnessed so far, we feel confident that we can make a few solid predictions.

CHAPTER EIGHT

What Lies Ahead

The future enters into us, in order to transform itself in us, long before it happens.
—Rainer Maria Rilke[1]

True to Rilke's words, the future of B2E is taking root inside most organizations already. We are the first to admit that we are early into this period of transformation—most of our case study organizations are only just beginning broad implementations of these new concepts. But like any revolution, the change will become evident only when we are no longer thinking about the change process itself.

For example, we believe that in the next five years, the world will stop talking about B2E in the same fashion that it stopped talking about electricity, telephones, and even the Internet. These mechanisms, so revolutionary and staggering at the outset, have become indispensable aspects of the way we live and work—so much so that they are nearly invisible in our mind's eye. The B2E portal will become as commonplace and invaluable as e-mail and cell phones, a standard organizational approach to how work gets done.

In a 2001 Forrester Research survey of Global 3500 companies, it is clear that most big companies have ambitious portal plans. Typical portals in these organizations will serve 10,000 employees or more, are content-centered, and integrate many disparate legacy systems. The survey found that organizational issues top the list of portal challenges, which is no surprise, considering the dramatic shifts in responsibilities and the reduction in layers of management that will result. Firms plan to spend big money on portals, but most don't plan to measure results with formal metrics. They simply understand that this transformation is crucial to doing business in the new millennium.

We believe that more and more large companies will lessen the reliance on strict ROI measures and begin to embrace what the Gartner Group calls *value on investment* (VOI). As Gartner pointed out in a November 2001 report,

> The view of value creation must change to accommodate the Internet and new business models such as collaborative commerce and other e-business value chains. These business models are harbingers of an economy in which intangible assets such as knowledge, information, and networks are the foundation of most new products and services.[2]

We agree with this assessment. Our thoughts and strategies about B2E are built on the notion that the intangibles will become quite tangible as companies experience vast improvements in communications, innovation, and, as a result, profitability.

As Gartner puts it,

> Soft initiatives create value by increasing organizational cohesion and the capacity and proficiency

178

to act, react, or transform. In many cases they also produce ROI. Over time, this value is increasingly the source of competitiveness, including increased value of brand, new and deeper core competencies, innovation, knowledge creation, increased depth and range of talent, and improved strength and diversity of human and technology networks.[3]

In fact, Gartner goes so far as to predict that by 2006, 50 percent of Fortune 1000 companies will identify an owner for workplace initiatives, formally track and manage intangible assets, and measure value creation, or VOI, on these initiatives.

Our experience tells us that companies that embrace B2E can expect to save between 30 and 50 percent of overhead costs by moving work to the web. This will happen because companies will be able to leverage the very things that make them great—the corporate wisdom, experience, product development, sales, channel expertise, and so on—and gain real speed and efficiency by moving work to the web.

We also believe the days of big corporate staffs are numbered. Inventories of assets are already being taken and decisions are being made about what is valuable and what can be jettisoned. Because of the efficiency and value in moving work to the web, companies simply won't need armies of staff people in an expensive headquarters building; the very face of bricks and mortar will change significantly along with the structure of organizations themselves.

Our case study companies understand all this in a visceral way. At places like the BBC, PwC, Ford, and HP, the very idea of standing still is simply not an option, because avoiding risks and embracing the status quo will mean failure in the long run. It is not enough to try to remain competitive with incremental baby steps. Moving forward is not an option but an obligation to all stakeholders. "People will have to learn new ways of working," states Greg Dyke, director-general of the BBC. Knowing this, however, doesn't ease the pain of the transformation.

Indeed, as you've read in these pages, the transformation of big organizations is difficult, often traumatic. So when companies make the commitment to B2E, they understand that this is territory that must be crossed in order to remain competitive into the future. "The portal is the connecting point for the essence of the process reinvention we're now going through," says HP's Carly Fiorina.

We have no doubt that there will be casualties along the way. Jacques Nasser, whose work toward a B2E-enabled Ford was both visionary and astute, nonetheless will not have the chance to see it through. Time will tell how Ford reacts to a change of leadership, but we are willing to bet that William Clay Ford, Jr., and his successors will come to understand the promise of B2E and revitalize the groundwork laid during Nasser's tenure.

With the B2E platform as a standard approach within many organizations, the power and lure of a single channel, a single logon, a simple excursion into identity management, there will come a time in the near future when few alternatives will be left. We are already overloaded with information coming at us via countless channels, and B2E and portals are critical in managing the flow. The B2E concept is already extending beyond the enterprise to include suppliers, partners, and customers as business practices become more and more web-enabled.

And in this way, the promise of mobile computing will finally reach its full potential as the myriad of computing devices—laptops, desktops, PDAs, cell phones—will merge into a single, personal environment. It won't matter anymore which device you are using and where you are located, the B2E environment will be accessible anytime, anywhere. This will eliminate the irritating, time-consuming switching back and forth between devices and computing environments, and there'll be far fewer compromises made around speed, resolution, and reliability. New advances in security and identity management will make all this far more practical and secure. And in this way, the B2E revolution will touch personal lives as well as work lives.

Cataclysmic events like the September 11 terrorist attacks refocused most Americans on issues surrounding work and family. But in truth, the pendulum had already been swinging in the direction of more fulfilling personal lives balanced with rewarding careers and commitments to employers. Technology is the underpinning of this accelerated change in the fundamental ways that people live and work. We believe our society is undergoing a shift in attitudes about work life, about the very concept of leaving home for extended periods in order to be paid, and about supporting a family. The enterprise portal concept dovetails perfectly with this new attitude.

As the technology has obviated the need for large groups of people gathered geographically in the same place in order for work to get done, people are experiencing a return-to-family metamorphosis. Corporate loyalty is difficult to foster in the face of massive layoffs, megamergers, and rising corporate consolidation. The portal permits a more balanced lifestyle by allowing employees to work from home and shift the focus to their personal lives, while retaining strong ties to the company that hosts the portal.

The concept of the *office* is being redefined, and we expect fewer mammoth facilities in centralized locations—the prototypical showplace headquarters—as people choose to work remotely. What we foresee is a time when people can work at home, juggle family responsibilities, and still remain productive. More and more workers are staying at or near home to accomplish the same things they once traveled long distances to achieve. A new sense of community is springing up around the family, and we believe that companies will need to accept and address this shift in attitude. The portal is the perfect medium to connect people's work lives with their personal lives. Businesses will have to rethink the very way they view employees and the workplace. Demand will increase for distance learning from universities and distance training from the companies themselves. The workplace of the future will be a B2E platform in someone's den, automobile, hotel, or remote office location.

People will be more responsible for their own careers and their own advancement than ever before. We're entering an age of initiative over intelligence. Armed with these new tools, workers will find resources and capabilities via the portal to change their lives in countless ways. Corporate cultures, once built upon proximity, will come to rely on the portal as the foundation for the company environment. Affiliations based on geographical location will be replaced by relationships fostered online, both within and outside the corporate setting. Employees who felt tremendous loyalty to HP, for example, are likely to bring new attitudes to the relationship. The HP portal will be My Portal, and the connection to the organization will be tempered by relationships that circle the individual in ways that extend beyond corporate boundaries. The equation might be something like this:

initiative × creativity + network connections = wealth

All of this implies that we will have to manage very differently and that organizational dynamics will be dramatically altered in ways we may not be able to predict just yet. Our own model at PwC is one that we foresee becoming more and more embraced in traditional companies. We are literally a partnership and therefore each of us must take ownership of the processes and the product. A customer to one of us is a customer to all and, as we reported in the PwC chapter (Chapter 5), the portal is already remaking the way we are able to provide services and value to these customers in new and innovative ways. This will become true for every organization in the future, whether it is a partnership or a traditional hierarchy. Work will get done differently and interactively with others on the web, spreading the wealth and responsibility in heretofore impossible ways.

Today, we are focused on moving single-user, role-based applications to the web. The next wave of applications will be collaborative and shared by groups or teams, which will design new products and share specifications with suppliers and partners around the world on a 24-7 basis. Business to everything will facilitate the creation of new products and new markets. The creation of innovative goods and services will accelerate far beyond what it is today. Pharmaceutical companies, for example, will be able to shorten research and product development cycles significantly by being able to share research, monitor results, and escalate regulatory processes by moving this work to the web in a secure way.

Information suppliers like PwC will escalate the value of their product lines exponentionally by offering access to global knowledge on an instant, as-needed basis that was heretofore impossible. Institutional knowledge and memory will be shared in ways that significantly improve the volume and quality of output. By transforming and simplifying the mundane administrative tasks via the portal, organizations like the BBC enhance the creative process, thereby freeing producers to make great programs without the burden of tiresome administrative tasks. Clients will be brought inside the walls, even the firewalls in some cases, to gain access to products and services in new, innovative ways.

And inevitably, the organization itself will change shape and form, embracing the long-awaited concepts of flexible and virtual workforces as the promise of the Internet is finally achieved.

THE SIEBEL MODEL

It has never been easy to threaten the corporate hierarchies that have been in place since the advent of the industrial revolution. But B2E is likely to be the linchpin to massive organizational change. Already companies like HP, Ford, and PwC are seeing a flattening of the organization, much like Tom Siebel has achieved at Siebel Systems.

In fact, Siebel may well be a model for the organization of the future. Because it actually sells customer relationship management (CRM) software aimed at enterprise-wide management of sales and customer service, Siebel has an obvious advantage over big companies in other industries. What Siebel has done within its own organization, however, cannot be minimized. Not all high-tech companies have been adept at using their own technology and often end up as the proverbial cobbler's children. However, the way Siebel operates takes full advantage of the web, and, regardless of its product set, there are lessons to be learned from the way it has moved work to the web. In this, Siebel offers a peek into a future that we believe is inevitable.

Siebel, with approximately 8,000 employees in 141 offices in 33 countries is the fastest-growing software company in history, surging from $0 to more than $2 billion in sales in just eight years. Founded in 1993, the organization relies upon IT and communication technology to establish and maintain relationships with its employees, as well as with its customers and partners. Tom Siebel, the company's founder, explains that the company spent two years building an enterprise application called Siebel Employee Relationship Management (ERM), which is used internally as the platform for all employees and all of their work. Inside the company, the application is called *my*Siebel. From any digital device, employees are able to access the information, applications, and other resources required in the course of a day. Nearly 90 percent of Siebel employees use *my*Siebel every day.

It is the sole source of intracompany news about the company, partners, competitors, and competitive information. Employees seeking data on budgets, planning, performance reviews, performance evaluations, quarterly objectives, budget variances, and objectives management need only log on and find what they are looking for. All of the firm's HR components are available as well, along with computer-aided training, courseware, and product training. The system handles all travel authorizations, travel expense reporting, and even directions to remote offices. As if all this weren't enough, all purchasing and procurements are authorized and executed on the system, and all marketing information, pricing, and advertising are online as well.

Though there is a common front page for the entire company, the rest of the system is entirely personalized to the individual and to that individual's department. What Siebel has done is create a working B2E environment at a time when most companies are either still thinking about it or just beginning to strive for that goal. The web isn't just an adjunct to their business processes, it *is* their business process. And the results are powerful and impressive.

"It allows us to communicate and reinforce a very rich corporate culture across our organization," Tom Siebel says. "By doing this, we can communicate the values that we hold important. And that, in the long run, is the final determinate of people's behavior."

Beyond that, the system, which Siebel says is more than a portal, offers "unusually robust visibility into revenue pipelines, expenses and predicted expenses, and an unusually robust ability to do planning and budgeting for the organization, the department, and the individual." Because of this, Siebel has been able to be especially responsive to market conditions at a time when most companies are struggling to adjust to rapidly shifting economic tides.

Siebel insists there is no magic to all of this. Successful companies in the new millennium are going to have to be able to control expenditure levels, adjust rapidly to marketplace changes, and modify people's behavior as necessary. The recession that began in 2001 moved swiftly and was accelerated dramatically by the September 11 attacks. Whole industries were caught in a sudden squeeze that left them unable to shift quickly to address the new economics.

With a well-conceived B2E strategy and the proper tools, most companies will be able to respond to market changes in far more effective ways in the future. Companies will need to be highly flexible in their ability to reallocate and redeploy resources, to resize organizations as necessary to meet the needs of changing competitive environments.

In 2000, for example, Siebel grew at a rate of 121 percent. By 2001, it was the second fastest-growing company in the United States. Entering 2001, the company, with revenues of $1.8 billion, set plans in place to grow to $4 billion and 15,000 people by 2002. Budget and revenue plans, along with lead generation, recruiting, training, and sales organizational restructure plans, were put in place and measurements were taken of organizational objectives.

Siebel was able to measure how the company was performing in precise increments not only by the quarter but by the day. In early March, the company knew that its growth plans were not going to be realized in the downward-shifting economy. "We replanned the business, rewrote departmental and company objectives, and individual objectives for eight thousand people," Siebel says. "We rewrote department operating budgets and resized the company. We took out two layers of management, reduced our headcount by 10 percent, rebudgeted, replanned, and redeployed all of our resources. It was all done by April 1, 2001."

As we said, Siebel has an advantage in using its own products to fuel its corporate makeup. We realize that most companies in other industries, from automotive to waste management, weren't built on such pragmatic and elegant foundations. The point of using Siebel as an example is to suggest that B2E can be achieved and is not simply a futuristic pipedream. The tools are out there from companies like Siebel and many others. What is crucial is the will to make it a reality.

There is no doubt that in order to build great companies, to bring exceptional, high-quality products to market, and to create organizations with high integrity and ethics that will attract the highest-quality people, companies have to embrace the B2E model. Building a global company where people want to work and where customer satisfaction reaches the highest levels requires these fundamental shifts in the use of IT and communication technology.

"Consider the swiftness with which we need to respond today," Tom Siebel says. "Things don't change in quarters, changes happen in weeks now, and you need to be able to readjust. It is clear to me that in five to ten years, one hundred percent of companies will rely extensively on these technologies to maintain their daily relationships with their employees."

PREPARING FOR THE CHANGES

Change doesn't happen because people ask for it. Change happens because circumstances dictate that it must occur. We believe that people's expectations about the workplace are already changing and will continue to change dramatically. What we foresee is the quickening of the pace toward reducing corporate hierarchies. There will be a fundamental shift away from rank, grade level, and seniority based on longevity or the old-boy corporate network, and an increase in the value of people with the ideas, knowledge, and creativity to make things happen. The best ideas will win, and the best people will be pushed forward and have an immediate impact on the organization. Talent won't have to wait 10 years to be recognized and rewarded.

We are seeing, as a result of B2E implementations, less staff focused on infrastructure such as HR, finance, IT, workplace services, and general administration, with a major move toward self-service. Hewlett-Packard has nearly eliminated the dozens of autonomous HR organizations spread around the company and replaced them with self-service options on the @hp portal. They are already realizing cost savings of more than 30 percent. The ideal marketplace, after all, is one in which decisions are made by the people using that market, working in that market, and trading in that market. Today, far too much time is spent trying to decide what is good for people. We expect a shift toward letting people decide what is good for them.

Indeed, the biggest impact will be felt among staff groups used to organize and disseminate information as they see fit. People whose sole task is finding information will see a rapid devaluing of their skills. New skill sets will be required. New job titles will emerge. Everyone will be in the media business, for example, and with the portal at their disposal, they will be publishers of their own domain. Certainly, this requires a new communications skill set. Having good ideas won't be enough. People will have to find ways to break through the clutter and get others' attention. Soaring above the noise will become the goal of B2E pioneers who undoubtedly will offer innovative and intriguing ways to get the message out in this new environment.

All of this will require a new skill set, which we call *portal communication.* Beyond visual and verbal skills, people will need to learn how to communicate effectively via the portal. In some ways, it will be a new language, and competency in this art will be in high demand. Influence and power will shift toward those who create, and they will shift away from those who collate. No surprise, there is risk in this scenario, and we are already seeing that risk manifest itself. Companies that don't make the transition smoothly will endure information chaos. Too much information thrown onto the portal will turn people off. Getting the right information to the right people in the right way will require skills rarely found in old-economy workers. As we described earlier in the book, we expect to see the embrace of a loose/tight organizational structure, in which companies are loose and open about letting people produce and share information but tight about making sure there are standards adhered to and guidelines and governance in place.

We are already seeing the fruits of this thinking in some of the early adopters of B2E, where employees are not only allowed, but encouraged, to customize their portal sites with webcams to their child's day care center, views of their stock portfolios, weather, traffic, and an unending list of applications that bring together work and personal lives.

In this flexible environment, we will have access to more information and more control over the information that we need. Organizations will need to strike a fine balance in this loose/tight environment. Rather than management deciding what employees need, B2E allows users to decide what they need for themselves and get it quickly. At HP and Ford, there is a strong emphasis on flexibility and allowing the portal to be customized for the individual. Some percentage of the portal real estate will be dictated by corporate staff, but much of the portal will be invented by the people who use it.

As we move toward this future, organizations must ask themselves some fundamental questions:

➜ Are we willing to create a senior-level portal executive position in order to make this work? Handing this off to the CIO will be a mistake because it will inevitably be labeled yet another technology project du jour.

➜ Have we thought through all the issues about governance to move confidently forward?

➜ In the quest toward globalization, how must the portal be constructed and implemented? Should there be one universal standard or local variations?

➜ Cultural decisions concerning benefits, education, compensation, and upward mobility that were once made by default will now need to be made specifically by each individual. How can companies assure that the right decisions will be made?

➜ Are the corporate IT systems and networks ready to handle the portal implementation?

➜ How will companies integrate the broad openness of the portal with the very real need for security and privacy?

➜ If the future is about me, the individual, how will the corporation retain enough conformity to make the process viable?

These are the issues with which B2E beginners are struggling as they push forward with their implementations. We hope this book has helped you formulate the answers to these questions. We have seen enough of both the pain and the promise of B2E to believe deeply that this is a viable path to the future. Woody Allen once joked that "Eighty percent of success is showing up." In the embrace of B2E, showing up is actually the toughest and most crucial step. Perhaps the hardest decision to make is the one that concludes: "Yes, we are going there." Strong leadership and a belief that the corporate transformation is inevitable and necessary is the only way to get an organization moving in this direction.

Uniting a thousand tribes is never easy. People resist, cynics appear, and roadblocks spring up along the way. As Carly Fiorina says, "The only way to deal with cynicism over time is to prove people wrong. The only way to prove people wrong is to keep at it." We believe that B2E is the corporate future. It is time to double-down and push ahead. We hope this book proves to be a useful guide along the way.

Notes

INTRODUCTION
1. Hammer, Michael, and James Champy, *Reengineering the Corporation.*
2. Friedman, Thomas L., *New York Times,* 27 July 2001.

CHAPTER ONE
1. Quotation by Francis Bacon published in *Bartlett's.*
2. Lohr, S., "New Economy," *New York Times,* 8 October 2001.
3. Lohr, S., "New Economy," *New York Times,* 8 October 2001.

CHAPTER THREE
1. Burrows, Peter, *Business Week,* 19 February 2001.

CHAPTER FOUR
1. Robinson, Edward, *Business2.0,* May 2001.
2. Robinson, Edward, *Business2.0,* May 2001.
3. Robinson, Edward, *Business2.0,* May 2001.
4. *Net Readiness.*

CHAPTER FIVE
1. Emerson, James C. (ed.), *Professional Services Review,* July/August 2001.

2. Emerson, James C. (ed.), *Professional Services Review,* July/August 2001.

CHAPTER SIX

1. British Broadcasting Corporation (BBC).

CHAPTER SEVEN

1. Bennis, Warren, *On Becoming a Leader,* Addison-Wesley, 1989.
2. Bennis, Warren, *On Becoming a Leader,* Addison-Wesley, 1989.

CHAPTER EIGHT

1. Quotation by Rilke, Rainer Maria published in *Bartlett's.*
2. The Gartner Group, November 2001.

Index